HOCKEY HOCKEY HOCKEY

THE ALL-NEW TRIVIA BOOK

DON WEEKES

GREYSTONE BOOKS
Douglas & McIntyre
Vancouver/Toronto

For Angela, Don and Jonathan

Greystone Books
A division of Douglas & McIntyre Ltd.
1615 Venables Street
Vancouver, British Columbia V5L 2H1

Canadian Cataloguing in Publication Data
Weekes, Don.
    Hockey, hockey, hockey

    ISBN 1-55054-452-7
    1. National Hockey League—Miscellanea. 2.Hockey—Miscellanea.
    I. Title.
GV847.W425 1995   796.962   C95-910361-9

Editing by Kerry Banks and Anne Rose
Design by Peter Cocking
Typesetting by Fiona MacGregor
Cover photo by Scott Levy/Bruce Bennett Studios
Printed and bound in Canada by Best Book Manufacturers
Printed on acid-free paper ∞

The publisher gratefully acknowledges the assistance of the Canada Council and of the British Columbia Ministry of Tourism, Small Business and Culture.

Don Weekes is a television producer and writer with CFCF 12 in Montreal. This is his sixth hockey trivia quiz book.

CONTENTS

PREFACE

There is no greater thrill in sport than witnessing the speed, grace and pure skill of a hockey player breaking through the neutral zone and bearing down on a goalie. His silver blades cut the ice, zigzagging through the blockade of forecheckers in his path. As his body tilts into the rush, his sweater ripples from the airstream off his back. The puck dances back and forth on his stick. The scraping of skates; the bruising contact of colliding bodies; and the crowd's roar. It's breathtaking, edge-of-your-seat stuff.

At the edge of the crease, the puck-stopper fixates on the skater's approach through a screen of defenders, correcting his position to the rush of attackers. This is the ultimate duel that defines the game. Who will commit first? Will the skater or the goalie force the other out of position?

The outcome can shatter or build team confidence with equal impact. During the 1995 Stanley Cup finals, the results of such play proved the turning point in New Jersey's four-game sweep over Detroit. The Devils' Scott Niedermayer picked up the puck and wheeled through the Red Wings' two-three forechecking system, strafing in on the league's best defenseman, Paul Coffey. Niedermayer launched the puck just wide of the net, deked behind Coffey and perfectly timed the room-service backboard rebound to whip a shot beyond a mesmerized Mike Vernon.

Niedermayer's dazzling gamesmanship raised the level of play in the series a notch. Even Detroit coach Scotty Bowman recognized the imminent demise of his highly skilled team in the wake of the Devils' awesome domination of play.

In this, our sixth book, we hope to share more of those moments. The scoring and puck-stopping plays legends are made of, the statistics that record breakers challenge, and the spirit and drama the game evokes for millions of fans.

Enjoy. Get more ice time.

DON WEEKES
July 1995

1

SHARPENING UP

The most important skill to master in hockey is skating. Players sharpen their skate blades every practice and game; some even sharpen between periods. The stainless steel blades, called runners, are designed for optimum balance and energy transfer to improve speed and turning power. Runners are usually replaced after about 100 sharpenings.

In this warm-up quiz, we hone your hockey trivia skills with a coast-to-coast sprint through a series of general questions, ranging from NHL offensive stats and trophy winners to more unusual topics, such as the origins of the hat trick, the 100th penalty-shot goal and POGs. Remember, all the questions have a logical answer, so pick the multiple choice statement that best fits. You'll need the perfect edge to make this cut.

(Answers are on page 7)

1.1 What was the average height and weight of NHL players in the 1990s?
A. Six foot, 190 pounds
B. Six foot one, 196 pounds
C. Six foot two, 202 pounds
D. Six foot two, 208 pounds

1.2 Who was the first European-trained player to win the Art Ross Trophy as NHL scoring leader?
A. Teemu Selanne
B. Jaromir Jagr
C. Stan Mikita
D. Peter Stastny

1.3 Which member of the 1995 Los Angeles Kings scored the goal that produced Wayne Gretzky's 2,500th NHL point?
A. Marty McSorley
B. Jari Kurri
C. Rob Blake
D. Rick Tocchet

1.4 According to *National Hockey League Official Rules*, the instigator of a fight automatically gets a game misconduct. He is also assessed a two-minute penalty if he is using:
A. Tape or other material on his hands
B. A mouth guard
C. An illegal stick
D. A face shield

1.5 How many NHL skaters wear face shields?
A. One in four skaters
B. One in five skaters
C. One in six skaters
D. One in seven skaters

1.6 Who was the first major "free agent" signed in the NHL? (It happened in 1975.)
A. Marcel Dionne
B. Ken Hodge
C. Bobby Orr
D. Frank Mahovlich

1.7 In what year did the NHL and the NHL Players' Association first grant a licence to produce POGs?
A. 1992
B. 1993
C. 1994
D. 1995

1.8 Who was the first player in NHL history to score 50 goals while playing for two teams in one season?
A. Dave Andreychuk
B. Jimmy Carson
C. Craig Simpson
D. Bob Carpenter

1.9 Which Flyer helped nickname the Eric Lindros-John LeClair-Mikael Renberg line "The Legion of Doom"?
A. Jim Montgomery
B. Rod Brind'Amour
C. Craig MacTavish
D. Ron Hextall

1.10 What is the average height and weight of The Legion of Doom line?
A. Six foot two, 201 pounds
B. Six foot two, 211 pounds
C. Six foot three, 221 pounds
D. Six foot three, 231 pounds

1.11 In a 1995 episode of "Seinfeld," the NBC TV sitcom featured a crazed New Jersey hockey fan wearing a Devils jersey. Which player's name and number made it to prime time?
A. Mike Peluso's No. 8
B. Martin Brodeur's No. 30
C. Claude Lemieux's No. 22
D. Scott Stevens's No. 4

1.12 **In which season is Scotty Bowman expected to overtake Al Arbour as the NHL bench boss with the most games coached?**
A. 1995–96
B. 1996–97
C. 1997–98
D. 1998–99

1.13 **The last names of three of the players listed below are similar in one way. Which name is different?**
A. Joel Otto
B. Gary Lupul
C. Dave Emma
D. Jiri Latal

1.14 **What high-ranking public position did the Canadian government offer Jean Béliveau in 1994?**
A. Executive director of Hockey Canada
B. Deputy minister of Fitness and Amateur Sport
C. Chairman of the Hockey Hall of Fame
D. Governor General of Canada

1.15 **After Wayne Gretzky, who is the youngest Hart Trophy winner (league MVP) in NHL history?**
A. Mario Lemieux
B. Eric Lindros
C. Bobby Orr
D. Bryan Trottier

1.16 **Hat trick is a term borrowed from cricket. How was it introduced to hockey?**
A. By a Toronto hat store owner
B. By an NHL referee who wore a cap
C. By a Detroit goal judge
D. By a Boston team physician who played cricket

1.17 Who is the only NHL rookie to score 100 points, and not win the Calder Trophy as top freshman?
A. Joe Juneau
B. Neal Broten
C. Larry Murphy
D. Steve Yzerman

1.18 Between 10 to 25 penalty shots have been called on average each year in the NHL since 1934–35, the season the rule was introduced. In what year was the NHL's 100th penalty-shot goal scored? (And name the scorer.)
A. 1953
B. 1963
C. 1973
D. 1983

1.19 Which rookie led his team in scoring during 1995's 48-game season?
A. Anaheim's Paul Kariya
B. Edmonton's David Oliver
C. Quebec's Peter Forsberg
D. Ottawa's Radek Bonk

1.20 After Bruce McNall filed for bankruptcy in 1994, who bought his half share of the 1909 Honus Wagner baseball card the former Kings owner and Wayne Gretzky purchased together for $451,000?
A. Gretzky's father, Walter Gretzky
B. Gretzky himself
C. Gretzky's close friend and agent, Mike Barnett
D. The Baseball Hall of Fame in Cooperstown, N.Y.

1.21 **How often has Dave Andreychuk changed his shoulder pads in the last 10 years?**
A. Never
B. Once
C. At least once each season
D. Twice each season

1.22 **How many *fewer* goals did Eric Lindros score than Jaromir Jagr to lose the 1995 scoring race?**
A. One goal
B. Two goals
C. Three goals
D. Four goals

1.23 **How many times has an NHL scoring championship been decided by total goals, after two players recorded equal regular-season point totals?**
A. Once, 1995
B. Three times
C. Four times
D. Five times

1.24 **Where did Phil Esposito finish in the NHL point standings the seasons prior to and following his trade from Chicago to Boston in 1967–68?**
A. Espo finished second as a Blackhawk in 1966–67; second as a Bruin in 1967–68
B. Espo finished second as a Blackhawk in 1966–67; seventh as a Bruin in 1967–68
C. Espo finished seventh as a Blackhawk in 1966–67; second as a Bruin in 1967–68
D. Espo finished seventh as a Blackhawk in 1966–67; seventh as a Bruin in 1967–68

1.25 What is the most number of games ever played by an NHLer during one regular season?
A. 86 games
B. 87 games
C. 88 games
D. 89 games

SHARPENING UP
Answers

1.1 B. Six foot one, 196 pounds
The average NHL player's size has steadily increased over the past two decades. What was once considered big (six feet, 190 pounds) is now considered below average, as teams look for larger, more mobile players to out-skate, out-reach and out-muscle the opposition. Hockey, according to many, is a hitting game. Throw your weight around and you throw your opposition off his game. Coupled with the right offensive strategies, it could decide championships.

1.2 B. Jaromir Jagr
Although Czechoslovakian-born Stan Mikita won the NHL's scoring race four times in the 1960s, he never played professionally in Europe. One generation later, Mikita's fellow countryman, Jagr, a Czech star in his native city, Kladno, defected to the NHL in 1990 and claimed the scoring title in 1995's 48-game season. Jagr netted 32 goals and 38 assists for 70 points to become the NHL's first European-trained Art Ross winner.

1.3 C. Rob Blake

On April 17, 1995, Gretzky reached the 2,500-point plateau with an assist on a Blake goal before 20,010 fans at Calgary's Olympic Saddledome. With the Kings buzzing on a first-period power play, Gretzky feathered a short pass back to Blake stationed at the Flames blue-line. The Los Angeles D-man fired a high slap shot, which hit goalie Rick Tabaracci before rolling up and over his shoulder into the net. The historic assist was cheered wildly by Flames fans, for whom the night ended happily: Calgary defeated the Kings 5–2. Gretzky hit the 2,500-point mark with 813 goals and 1,687 assists in 1,165 career games.

1.4 D. A face shield

Veteran goon Tiger Williams personally lobbied for Rule 54 (a), which states that in addition to a game misconduct, fight instigators who wear face shields shall also be assessed an additional minor penalty. The rule punishes instigators who use face guards because of their unfair advantage in a fight situation. Shields offer extra protection and can badly cut an opponent's fists.

1.5 C. One in six skaters

About 16 per cent, or 90 players (out of 572 NHLers), use face/eye protection, such as Itech's poly-carbonate plastic shield. Some players, including Jaromir Jagr and Luc Robitaille, wear them from day one; others, like Ron Francis, wait until an injury occurs. When Eric Lindros injured an eye in 1995, he used a shield on doctor's orders. But after a couple of games, he went back to barefacing it. The reasons most often given for *not* wearing shields? Too warm, poor visibility and the "macho/toughness" factor.

1.6 A. Marcel Dionne

According to a 1975 agreement between the NHL and the players' association, any player whose contract expires can move to a new team, provided equal compensation is awarded to the player's former club. On June 23, 1975, Dionne became the first big-name free agent in history after signing with Los Angeles. The Kings gave up Don Maloney, Terry Harper and a second-round draft choice as compensation to Detroit for Dionne and Bart Crashley.

1.7 D. 1995

POGs, for anyone who missed the first half of the 1990s, are cardboard discs resembling old milk bottle caps that kids stack up and try to flip by throwing a "kini"— a heavier POG made of plastic—on the pile. The POGs that flip over after the toss become "yours." It's an old-fashioned game that disappeared when milk bottles were replaced by cartons. Since its revival in 1991, the POG craze has swept across North America. The NHL POGs feature a player's picture and career stats, much like hockey cards. The first 376-piece set was issued in January 1995.

1.8 C. Craig Simpson

Only two NHLers have ever been traded during a 50-goal season: Simpson and Andreychuk. After potting 13 goals in 21 games for Pittsburgh in 1987-88, Simpson was dealt to Edmonton (November 24, 1987), where he netted another 43 goals in 59 matches for a Penguin-Oiler 56-goal total. Andreychuk is the only other 50-goal man with a two-team split—his came in 1992–93, between Buffalo (29 goals) and Toronto (25 goals).

1.9 A. Jim Montgomery

"The Legion of Doom" nickname developed out of a Montgomery comment made to Les Bowen of the *Philadelphia Daily News* at a Flyer practice, just a few days after the big trade. In his observations about the line's size, Montgomery, a huge wrestling fan, remarked that the new Philly forward unit resembled the Legion of Doom, a prowrestling tag team. Many other nicknames were suggested (Bob's Big Boys, among them), but nothing rivalled Montgomery's characterization of the biggest line of 1995.

1.10 C. Six foot three, 221 pounds

Considered the game's largest regular forward line, The Legion of Doom averages six feet three inches and 221 pounds—two inches taller and 25 pounds heavier than the regular NHLer. Together, Lindros (six foot four, 229 pounds), LeClair (six foot two, 215 pounds) and Renberg (six foot two, 218 pounds) measure 18 feet, eight inches tall and weigh 662 pounds.

1.11 B. Martin Brodeur's No. 30

During the "Seinfeld" episode, Elaine dates a hockey fan who turns out to be a "face painter," someone who, in this case, paints his face green and red for Devils games. The fan also wears a New Jersey sweater with the No. 30 and the name "BRODEUR" on the back. Interestingly, the program aired the evening prior to Brodeur recording his third shutout against the Boston Bruins in the Eastern Conference quarter-finals. It marked only the fifth time a goalie posted three SOs in a best-of-seven format since 1939.

1.12 A. 1995-96

After 1995's 48-game schedule, Bowman, with 1,572 games coached, was just 34 matches behind Arbour's record total of 1,606. Bowman will take over the NHL record for most games coached in 1995–96.

1.13 C. Dave Emma

Here's a neat word puzzle. Emma is different than the other surnames because Otto, Lupul and Latal are palindromes—words spelled the same way forwards and backwards. Palindromes are highly uncommon, not only in hockey, but in baseball, which has at least eight, including the Cubs' Dave Otto and Robb Nen of the Marlins, who pitched in the same game in 1994. Otto, Lupul and Latal have all played against each other, too.

1.14 D. Governor General of Canada

In September 1994, Béliveau was invited to dinner at 24 Sussex Drive, the Canadian prime minister's Ottawa residence. After dessert, Prime Minister Jean Chrétien asked the legendary Béliveau to become Canada's next Governor General, the same position once held in the 1890s by Lord Stanley, donator of the Cup Béliveau won 10 times while playing with the Canadiens. His country asked, but Béliveau, 64, declined, stating that family matters in Montreal prevented him from taking the five-year Ottawa job.

1.15 C. Bobby Orr

Gretzky won the first of nine MVP honours in his first NHL season, 1979-80, when he was just 19 years, five months old. The next youngest MVP is Orr, who at 21 years, nine months of age, won the Hart after posting an incredible 120-point season in 1969–70, the first time an NHL defenseman broke the 100-point barrier. Lindros snagged his 1995 Hart at age 22 years, four months; Lemieux, in 1988, at 22 years, eight months; and Trottier, in 1979, at 22 years, 11 months.

1.16 A. By a Toronto hat store owner

Hockey's hat trick tradition began in a small Toronto hat store called Sammy Taft, World Famous Hatter. One night in the 1940s, Hawks winger Alex Kaleta dropped by before game time to purchase a hat. Taft offered Kaleta the hat gratis if he scored three goals that night. Sure enough, Kaleta potted three goals. Taft kept his promise and from that moment on, every player scoring a hat trick at Maple Leaf Gardens received a courtesy hat from the World Famous Hatter. Taft stopped the tradition in the 1950s.

1.17 A. Joe Juneau

While Winnipeg's Teemu Selanne tore up the league to establish a rookie record of 76 goals and 132 points, Juneau also turned a few heads by potting 102 points (32G–70A). It's the highest point total ever scored by a rookie who didn't win Calder honours; and that includes Broten (98 points in 1982), Murphy (76 points in 1985) and Yzerman (87 points in 1984).

1.18 D. 1983

The league's 100th penalty-shot goal was scored on March 14, 1983, by Calgary's Paul Reinhart on New Jersey goalie Ron Low. Between 1934 and 1983, 276 penalty shots were called with 100 goals resulting, a scoring average of 36.2 per cent.

1.19 A. Anaheim's Paul Kariya

During 1995's abbreviated season, Kariya was the only rookie to lead his team in scoring with a 18–21–39 record, 10 points more than teammate Shaun Van Allen. Kariya was selected fourth overall in the 1993 NHL entry draft, following two seasons split between Canada's national Junior and Olympic teams and the University of Maine Black Bears, where he became the first freshman to win the Hobey Baker award as top U.S. college player (1992–93). That year, Kariya helped the Black Bears win the NCAA national championship by scoring three assists in the third period of the championship game to lead Maine from a 4–2 deficit to a 5–4 victory over Lake Superior State. Kariya was also a member of Canada's gold-medal-winning team at the 1992–93 World Junior Championships.

1.20 B. Gretzky himself

Originally bought in a partnership deal between McNall and Gretzky for $451,000 (the highest purchase price ever for a baseball card), the 1909 Honus Wagner card is now owned 100 per cent by Gretzky, who purchased McNall's half-ownership of the card from bankruptcy trustees for $225,500. Gretzky's 1909 Honus Wagner card is considered to be the highest-graded card of the 40 Wagners in existence.

1.21 A. Never

After 10 seasons, Andreychuk's battle-worn shoulder pads have probably been cross-checked and battered more often, and have absorbed more sweat and required more restitching or replacement parts, than any other piece of hockey equipment in the NHL today. Under constant repair, the padding is threadbare, the metal fasteners rusted and the once-white shell has turned a brownish-yellow. Still, the beat-up pads protecting Andreychuk's big shoulders fit like a comfortable shoe: not too attractive, but worth the maintenance after a lifetime of wear.

1.22 C. Three goals

Each tied with 70 points apiece after the 48-game schedule, but Lindros lost the scoring title to Jagr, outgoaled 32 to 29. Battling goal-for-goal throughout the season, the two superstars settled the championship only after Jagr scored four goals and an assist in the final three games, while Lindros sat out the last two matches with an eye injury. If the top two players share the lead in total points after regular-season play, the winner is determined by most goals.

1.23 B. Three times

The best evidence against the opinion that an assist is just as important as a goal? Look at Andy Bathgate, Wayne Gretzky and Eric Lindros, who all lost the NHL scoring title despite tying in total points. Bobby Hull, Marcel Dionne and Jaromir Jagr each scored more goals in those respective years.

GOALS-ARE-BETTER-THAN-ASSISTS CHAMPIONS					
Year	Player	GP	G	A	PTS
1961–62	Bobby Hull	70	50	34	84
	Andy Bathgate	70	28	56	84
1979–80	Marcel Dionne	80	53	84	137
	Wayne Gretzky	79	51	86	137
1995	Jaromir Jagr	48	32	38	70
	Eric Lindros	46	29	41	70

1.24 C. Espo finished seventh as a Blackhawk in 1966–67; second as a Bruin in 1967–68

Esposito was unquestionably the best player in the Boston-Chicago swap that sent him, Ken Hodge and Fred Stanfield to the Bruins for Pit Martin, Gilles Marotte and Jack Norris. Prior to the trade, Esposito had 61 points—seventh best in the league (and the fourth Hawk in the NHL's top seven). After the deal to Boston, he exploded, finishing second with 84 points, just three fewer than Art Ross Trophy-winner Stan Mikita. The coming years would prove how disastrous the trade was for Chicago. Within three years, it turned the hapless Bruins into Stanley Cup winners and transformed the Blackhawks from first-place finishers to cellar-dwellers. Esposito, the first player to break the 100-point barrier, won five scoring titles (and finished second to Bobby Orr twice) during his eight-year tenure with Boston.

1.25 A. 86 games

The only way to play more games than in an 84-game schedule is through a trade, moving mid-season from a team ahead in games played to a club behind in the sked. Over the years, many traded NHLers have outplayed the regular-season schedules by a game, but only two (at last count) have played two extra matches since the 84-game schedule began in 1992–93. Jimmy Carson dressed for 86 games in 1992–93, playing 52 for Detroit and 34 for the Kings; Bob Kudelski split his 1993–94 season between Ottawa (42) and Florida (44).

GAME 1

THE PINWHEEL PUCK

In this pinwheel game each word joins in the same way as a regular crossword. Starting at square number one, work clockwise around the four concentric rings or towards the centre along the spokes, filling in the correct answer from the clues below. Each answer begins with the last letter of the previous word. Determine word length by using the clue numbers. (The answer to number one is 16 letters long since the next clue is number five.)

AROUND

1. Traditional post-season celebration (3 words)
5. _____ "Moose" Vasko
7. Player lineup or team _____
9. "The Russian _____"
11. Phil Esposito's nickname as a general manager
13. Detroit's Reed _____
16. Lost all feeling
17. The All-Star _____
18. The Isles' Rich _____
20. Goalie Andy _____
22. Brave, lots of _____
23. "_____ for five"
24. Camille "The _____" Henry
25. 1950 Red Wing, Tony _____
26. Part of leg: _____ injury
27. Toronto's Ron _____
28. _____ Cleghorn
29. Waste time: "_____ up the clock"
30. Toronto legend and donut-maker (2 words)
31. Minnesota _____ Stars
32. Get good: "Get the _____ of it"
33. 1940's Leaf, _____ Bodnar
34. "_____ tall"
35. Detroit's _____ Ullman
36. Older adviser
37. Offensive up-ice term
38. Hawk goalie Glenn _____
39. Montreal's Elmer _____
40. Old radio show: "_____ Stove League"

41. Make a player fall
42. Yank or "_____ the goalie"
43. _____ Odelein
44. Appoint by vote
45. Lionel Conacher, "The Big _____"
46. Team proprietor
47. 1940s New York goalie, Chuck _____
48. Detroit's _____ Kelly
49. Outmanoeuvre: "____ out of position"
50. 1960's Ranger, _____ Ingarfield
51. Defeat
52. Slow video movement

TOWARDS CENTRE

2. _____ Maple Leafs
3. Detroit's Steve _____
4. Street corner of old Habs Forum, St. Catherine and _____
6. D-man Rod _____
8. To save or _____ the game
10. Bad defeat, a massacre
12. Fantastic
13. At home, _____ _____ advantage (2 words)
15. Toronto's Darryl _____
17. 1951 Cup hero, Toronto's Bill _____
19. New York _____
21. Province of Canada

17

2

RECORD BREAKERS AND AMERICAN FIRSTS

Who scored the fastest five-goal game from the start of a career? Remember Don Murdoch? Murdoch made his debut in high-flying style, popping the NHL's fastest five-goal game from a career start on October 12, 1976—in just his fourth game. The only other NHL rookie to notch a five-goal game was Howie Meeker in 1947, but he did it in his 27th game. In this chapter we bombard you with NHL records of all sorts, including a few American firsts worthy of recognition.

(Answers are on page 22)

2.1 After Wayne Gretzky and Mike Bossy, which player scored the most goals in his first three NHL seasons?
A. Mario Lemieux
B. Brett Hull
C. Pavel Bure
D. Luc Robitaille

2.2 Bobby Carpenter was the first American-born player to go directly from high school hockey into the NHL. What other NHL "first" did he accomplish?
A. The first American to compile a 100-point season
B. The first American to play 1,000 games
C. The first American to compile a 50-goal season
D. The first American drafted first overall

2.3 **Who was the first NHL rookie to score 100 points?**
A. Guy Lafleur
B. Peter Stastny
C. Bobby Clarke
D. Denis Savard

2.4 **What is the most number of penalty minutes assessed to one player during a single NHL season?**
A. 300 to 350 minutes
B. 350 to 400 minutes
C. 400 to 450 minutes
D. 450 to 500 minutes

2.5 **What is the fastest time one player has scored four goals?**
A. Less than three minutes
B. Between three and five minutes
C. Between five and seven minutes
D. More than seven minutes

2.6 **Who was the first American-born player to score 1,000 points? (And in what season?)**
A. Joe Mullen
B. Neal Broten
C. Phil Housley
D. Pat LaFontaine

2.7 **Who finished third behind Wayne Gretzky and Marcel Dionne in the 1980–81 scoring race?**
A. Mike Bossy
B. Peter Stastny
C. Dave Taylor
D. Kent Nilsson

2.8 Among NHLers who spent their entire careers with one team, who played the most games?
A. Chicago's Stan Mikita
B. Montreal's Bob Gainey
C. Buffalo's Gilbert Perreault
D. Detroit's Alex Delvecchio

2.9 What two generations of an American family succeeded in winning Olympic gold medals in ice hockey?
A. The Morrow family
B. The Christian family
C. The Pavelich family
D. The Broten family

2.10 What is the NHL record for the highest plus/minus rating by one skater in a single game?
A. A plus-5 rating
B. A plus-7 rating
C. A plus-9 rating
D. A plus-11 rating

2.11 Jari Kurri was the first European-trained player to score 50 goals in a single NHL season. Who was the second?
A. Peter Stastny
B. Hakan Loob
C. Kent Nilsson
D. Mats Naslund

2.12 Who was the first U.S.-born player to score five goals in an NHL game?
A. Mark Pavelich
B. Neal Broten
C. Bob Carpenter
D. Brian Lawton

2.13 How many games did St. Louis forward Tony Twist play from the start of his NHL career before scoring his first goal?
A. Less than 50 games
B. Between 50 and 100 games
C. Between 100 and 150 games
D. More than 150 games

2.14 Besides Bobby Hull, who is the other player to score 50 goals in both the NHL and WHA?
A. Michel Goulet
B. Mark Napier
C. Blaine Stoughton
D. Wayne Gretzky

2.15 Who was the first player to score 200 goals for two different NHL teams?
A. Norm Ullman in Detroit and Toronto
B. Frank Mahovlich in Toronto and Montreal
C. Phil Esposito in Boston and New York
D. Lanny McDonald in Toronto and Calgary

2.16 Who was the first NHLer to reach the 200-goal plateau playing for a 1967 expansion team?
A. Minnesota's Bill Goldsworthy
B. Philadelphia's Bobby Clarke
C. St. Louis' Red Berenson
D. Philadelphia's Rick MacLeish

2.17 What penalty-minute leader scored the most goals (in the same season he led the league in PIM)?
A. Ted Lindsay
B. Dave Williams
C. Stan Mikita
D. Bob Probert

2.18 Who was the first U.S.-born player to score 50 goals and 50 assists in one NHL season?

A. Bob Carpenter
B. Pat LaFontaine
C. Jimmy Carson
D. Joe Mullen

RECORD BREAKERS AND AMERICAN FIRSTS
Answers

2.1 **C. Pavel Bure**

The Russian Rocket blasted off into the NHL stratosphere of records, becoming the third-highest goal scorer in his first three seasons by notching 34, 60 and 60 goals between 1991 and 1994. On his dazzling flight path to 154 goals, Bure earned much more than the 1992 Calder Trophy (top rookie) and "human highlight reel" credentials as goal-scoring leader of 1993–94 by signing a new six-year, $25-million contract with the Canucks. Not too shabby, considering he began his career as a sixth-round (113th overall) pick in the 1989 entry draft.

Player	Years	Total Games	Seasons 1st	2nd	3rd	Total Goals
W. Gretzky	1979–82	239	51	55	92	198
M. Bossy	1977–80	228	53	69	51	173
P. Bure	1991–94	224	34	60	60	154
J. Nieuwendyk	1987–90	231	51	51	51	147
M. Lemieux	1984–87	215	43	48	54	145
B. Hull	1985–88	223	32	41	72	145
L. Robitaille	1986–89	237	45	53	46	144

THE NHL'S THREE-YEAR GOAL-SCORING WONDERS

2.2 C. The first American to compile a 50-goal season

Carpenter, from Beverly, Massachusetts, claimed two NHL "American firsts," jumping from St. John's High School in Massachusetts, in 1981, to the Washington Capitals where, four years later (in 1984–85), he notched 53 goals to become the first U.S.-born 50-goal scorer.

2.3 B. Peter Stastny

Still considered a rookie at 24, after several seasons with Slovan in his native Czechoslovakia, Stastny turned the NHL inside out in his debut season (39–70–109), potting his 100th point on a Michel Goulet goal on March 29, 1981. It was an NHL first for a rookie. (Wayne Gretzky, who scored 137 points in his freshman year, 1979–80, was not considered an NHL rookie because of his WHA service.)

2.4 D. 450 to 500 minutes

Few players, including even the toughest goons, have ever exceeded the 400 penalty-minute mark—and that includes heavyweights such as Marty McSorley, Bob Probert and Chris Nilan. But Dave "The Hammer" Schultz epitomized thuggery. His Broad Street Bullies style of playing equated ice-fighting to goal scoring. In 1974–75, Schultz hammered enough opponents to establish an NHL record of 472 penalty minutes—the equivalent of almost eight complete games in the box.

2.5 B. Between three and five minutes

Washington's Peter Bondra scored the NHL's four fastest goals by one player on February 5, 1994, when he netted four goals on four consecutive shots in just four minutes and 12 seconds, coming in a first period splurge at 14:44, 15:59, 16:30 and 18:56 against Tampa Bay's Darren Puppa.

2.6 A. Joe Mullen

Mullen is one of those athletes who defies logic.
Despite being the oldest regular-playing NHLer in 1995
at age 38, he continues to outscore his career average of
36 goals per season. In a physical sport that discrimi-
nates against smaller players, Mullen excels at only five
foot nine and 180 pounds; four inches shorter and 20
pounds lighter than the average player. And Mullen
only became an NHL regular at age 25, after escaping
one of New York's toughest 'hoods, Hell's Kitchen. Yet
despite the disadvantages and all the aches and pains
of a 14-year pro career, Mullen was the first American-
born player (and 42nd NHLer) to reach the lofty 1,000-
point plateau. It came on a four-point night against the
Panthers on February 7, 1995. After the 1995 abbreviated season, he was 13 goals shy of another NHL first for
an American: the 500-goal club.

2.7 D. Kent Nilsson

Nilsson's career year was 1980–81, when he trailed
Dionne by just four points and, like everyone else, was
miles behind the Great One—but far ahead of stars
such as Bossy, Taylor and Stastny. Originally drafted by
Atlanta, Swedish-born Nilsson spent two WHA years
with the Jets, before becoming a 40-goal NHL rookie
with the Flames in 1979–80. His puck wizardry earned
him the nickname "Magic Man." The following year his
soft hands turned everything he touched to gold as he
recorded a career-high 131 points. Nilsson retired in
1987 with 263 goals and 685 points in 547 NHL games,
and 214 points in 158 matches for the WHA Winnipeg
Jets. His attempted NHL comeback at 38 (after an eight-
year absence) lasted just six games in 1995, and produced one goal for Edmonton.

KENT NILSSON'S CAREER YEAR · 1980–81

Player	Team	GP	G	A	PTS	PIM
W. Gretzky	Edm.	80	55	109	164	28
M. Dionne	LA	80	58	77	135	70
K. Nilsson	**Cal.**	**80**	**49**	**82**	**131**	**26**
M. Bossy	NYI	79	68	51	119	32
D. Taylor	LA	72	47	65	112	130
P. Stastny	Que.	77	39	70	109	37

2.8   D. Detroit's Alex Delvecchio

Delvecchio leads all single-team NHLers with the most number of games played: 1,549 games over 24 consecutive years with the Red Wings organization from 1950 to 1974. In that time, Delvecchio was a horse, playing in 1,537 games out of a possible 1,580. He missed just 43 games during a 22-year stretch (22 scratches coming in 1956–57 alone)!

THE NHL'S SINGLE-TEAM/GAMES PLAYED LEADERS

Player	Team	Games	Years	G	A	Pts.
A. Delvecchio	Det	**1549**	24	456	825	1281
S. Mikita	Chi	**1394**	22	541	926	1467
H. Richard	Mon	**1256**	20	358	688	1046
G. Perreault	Buf	**1191**	17	512	814	1326
G. Armstrong	Tor	**1187**	21	296	417	713
B. Gainey	Mon	**1160**	16	239	262	501
B. Clarke	Phi	**1144**	15	358	852	1210

2.9   B. The Christian Family
It's a "like father, like son" story that makes Uncle Sam proud. What are the chances of two generations of one family winning the only two Olympic gold medals claimed by America in ice hockey? For the Christian family of Warroad, Minnesota, the 1980 Winter Games produced their own "miracle on ice" when son Dave became the second generation to strike Olympic gold, 20 years after his father, Bill, and uncle Roger won in 1960. Both U.S. victories were clear upsets. Each happened on American ice, in Squaw Valley, California, in 1960, and in Lake Placid, New York, in 1980.

2.10   C. A plus-9 rating
On February 10, 1993, Calgary's Theoren Fleury established a single game NHL record by posting a plus-9 rating in the Flames 13–1 victory over San Jose. Fleury victimized the Sharks' Arturs Irbe and Jeff Hackett, scoring a goal and five assists. He was also on the ice for three other Calgary goals, and on the bench when Johan Garpenlov potted the lone Shark goal. (A skater receives a plus-1 for each goal scored by his team when he's playing and a minus-1 for a goal-against if he's on-ice.)

2.11   B. Hakan Loob
Kurri, from Helsinki, Finland, had four 50-goal seasons with the Edmonton Oilers before Swedish-native Loob became the second European-trained NHLer to hit the half-century mark. Loob reached the 50-goal plateau in 1987-88, potting goal number 50 against Minnesota's Don Beaupre in a 4–1 Calgary win on April 3, 1988. It came on a Flame power play with just 3:05 remaining in the last game of the 80-game schedule.

2.12 A. Mark Pavelich

The first time an American-born player scored five or more goals in a single game was on February 23, 1983, when second-year Ranger Mark Pavelich, from Eveleth, Minnesota, bombed Whaler goalie Greg Millen five times in an 11–3 wipe-out. To date, no other American has repeated Pavelich's feat.

2.13 D. More than 150 games

It was a long time comin' for tough guy Tony Twist. In fact, 181 games is the longest any NHLer has ever waited from the start of his career to score a goal. Twist went without a goal from 1989 to 1995, playing first in St. Louis (28 games) and then in Quebec (151 games). His 1995 return to the Blues sparked an "offensive surge" as Twist scored his landmark goal in just the second game of the season (January 21, 1995) against Vancouver's Kay Whitmore. It was his 181st NHL game. Obviously, Twist liked the Blues. He scored his second career goal five games later!

2.14 C. Blaine Stoughton

Stoughton was one of the few WHAers, other than marquee players such as Gretzky, Howe and Hull, who had the talent to cut it in the NHL. Originally with Pittsburgh and Toronto, Stoughton blossomed in the WHA, scoring 52 goals with Cincinnati in 1976–77. After the NHL-WHA merger in 1979, he returned to the NHL a seasoned veteran and notched two +50-goal seasons— 56 goals to share the league lead in 1979–80, and 52 goals (the sixth-best total) in 1981–82. Stoughton is still Hartford's only 50-goal man.

2.15 D. Lanny McDonald in Toronto and Calgary

Only two players have ever scored 200 goals with two NHL teams. While Esposito, Ullman and Mahovlich just missed with their respective clubs, McDonald netted 219 goals as a Maple Leaf (1973 to 1979) and 215 goals with Calgary (1981 to 1989). Wayne Gretzky is the only other 200-200 scorer in NHL history, a feat he realized in 1993–94 after amassing 583 and 231 goals between Edmonton and Los Angeles.

2.16 A. Minnesota's Bill Goldsworthy

Hard-nosed yet gifted, Goldsworthy played a rugged brand of hockey that earned him the ice space he needed to rack up points. He was Minnesota's first legitimate star, a crowd favourite who could score goals as easily as land punches. Goldsworthy became the first 200-goal man from a post-1967 expansion team on March 10, 1974, when he whipped home his 38th goal of the season in an 8–1 romp over St. Louis. In 670 North Stars games, he totalled 267 goals and 506 points. Goldsworthy's No. 8 was retired by Minnesota in 1992.

2.17 B. Dave Williams

In 1980–81, Williams recorded a league-high 343 penalty minutes and scored 35 goals, the most season goals for a penalty leader in NHL history. Williams only holds the lead in this category because of Vic Hadfield, 1963–64's penalty leader. Hadfield accumulated 151 penalty minutes, just five minutes more than Stan Mikita, who registered 146 minutes in the box while scoring 39 goals—enough to top Williams' record 35 tallies.

THE NHL'S TOP GOAL-SCORING PENALTY LEADERS

Goals	Player	Team	Season	PIM
35	Dave Williams	Van	1980–81	343
29	Bob Probert	Det	1987–88	398
29	Joe Lamb	Ott	1929–30	119
28	Maurice Richard	Mon	1952–53	112
23	Billy Boucher	Mon	1922–23	52
22	Ted Lindsay	Det	1958–59	184
21	Chris Nilan	Mon	1984–85	358

2.18 C. Jimmy Carson

At 18, Carson proved quickly what all the hockey scouts had predicted at the 1986 NHL draft: this American kid (from Southfield, Michigan), who was rewriting the scoring records of the Quebec Major Junior Hockey League, would be the next NHL wunderkind. A year after Carson's 79-point rookie season with the Kings, he turned up the boosters and rocketed to a 107-point year in 1987–88, ripping 55 goals and 52 assists to become the first American-born player to record 50-and-50 in one season.

GAME 2

ROOKIES—THE HONOUR ROLL

In this game, place the Calder Trophy winners and runner-up rookies listed below in the correct year, opposite the competition they either defeated or placed second to in balloting for Rookie of the Year honours. To guide you, Calder winners and runners-up are indicated by a "W" and "R" respectively.

(Solutions are on page 115)

Mario Lemieux(W)   Ron Hextall(R)   Steve Yzerman(R)
Gary Suter(W)   Sergei Makarov(W)   Trevor Linden(R)
Sergei Fedorov(R)   Peter Forsberg(W)   Teemu Selanne(W)
Joe Nieuwendyk(W)   Nicklas Lidstrom(R)   Jason Arnott(R)

	Winner	**Runner-up**
1995	_____	Jim Carey
1994	Martin Brodeur	_____
1993	_____	Joe Juneau
1992	Pavel Bure	_____
1991	Ed Belfour	_____
1990	_____	Mike Modano
1989	Brian Leetch	_____
1988	_____	Ray Sheppard
1987	Luc Robtaille	_____
1986	_____	Wendel Clark
1985	_____	Chris Chelios
1984	Tom Barrasso	_____

3

THE PUCK STOPPERS

Just as our parents told us of legendary goaltending greats, such as Sawchuk, Hall and Plante, one day we will brag to our children about Brodeur, Hasek and Roy. The 1990s have produced a stable of netminders equal to any in the annals of hockey. Although the game has changed since the old days, making some goaltending records impossible to beat (like Hall's 502-game ironman record and Sawchuk's 103-shutout career mark), the new kids in the crease are setting their own standards, creating a whole new puck-stopping legacy.

(Answers are on page 34)

3.1 How much did Stanley Cup-winning goalie Martin Brodeur earn (before his case went to arbitration) during 1995's lockout-shortened season?
A. Less than $100,000
B. $500,000
C. $1 million
D. $2 million

3.2 Name the only goalie in NHL history who didn't record a single shutout the year he won the Vezina Trophy (league's top netminder) single-handedly.
A. Ron Hextall
B. Pelle Lindbergh
C. Johnny Bower
D. Billy Smith

3.3 Into the 1995–96 season, which European-trained goalie had the most NHL career games played?
A. Peter Sidorkiewicz
B. Arturs Irbe
C. Pelle Lindbergh
D. Dominik Hasek

3.4 Who was the first goalie in league history to assist on two goals in one game?
A. Jacques Plante
B. Ed Giacomin
C. Grant Fuhr
D. John Davidson

3.5 Which Canadian goalie refused to allow his likeness to appear on a Swedish postage stamp?
A. Corey Hirsch
B. Trevor Kidd
C. Sean Burke
D. Craig Billington

3.6 What Washington goalie refused to allow his bad-luck sister to watch his games in person?
A. Rick Tabaracci
B. Don Beaupre
C. Jim Carey
D. Pete Peeters

3.7 What Ranger goalie wore jersey No. 00 for one season?
A. Mike Richter
B. John Vanbiesbrouck
C. Gump Worsley
D. John Davidson

3.8 Which Colorado Rockies player accidentally scored into his own empty net, thereby crediting Islander goalie Billy Smith with the NHL's first goal by a netminder?

A. Lanny McDonald
B. Barry Beck
C. Rob Ramage
D. Wilf Paiement

3.9 How many shots did New York goalie Ken "Tubby" McAuley face in a record 15–0 loss to Detroit on January 23, 1944?

A. 28
B. 38
C. 48
D. 58

3.10 Among the 540 players drafted in the first round between 1969 and 1995, how many were goalies?

A. Less than 10
B. Between 10 and 20
C. Between 20 and 30
D. More than 30

3.11 What is Patrick Roy's favourite trading card set?

A. 1952–53 Parkhurst
B. 1912–13 Sweet Caporal
C. 1963–64 Topps
D. 1986–87 O-Pee-Chee

3.12 How many total minutes in nets did Glenn Hall play during his NHL-record 552 consecutive game streak?

A. Less than 30,000 minutes
B. 31,000 to 32,000 minutes
C. 32,000 to 33,000 minutes
D. More than 33,000 minutes

3.13 **What goalie made headlines by calling the Maple Leafs "undeserving" Stanley Cup contenders in the playoff finals of 1947?**
A. The Canadiens' Bill Durnan
B. The Bruins' Frank Brimsek
C. The Red Wings' Harry Lumley
D. The Maple Leafs' Turk Broda

3.14 **Who was the first goalie since Bernie Parent in 1973–74 to record a goals-against average below 2.00?**
A. Toronto's Felix Potvin
B. Montreal's Patrick Roy
C. Buffalo's Dominik Hasek
D. New Jersey's Martin Brodeur

THE PUCK STOPPERS
Answers

3.1 **A. Less than $100,000**
Brodeur, NHL Rookie of the Year in 1994 and the centre-piece of the New Jersey Devils' 1995 Stanley Cup championship team, was the lowest-paid full-time NHLer in 1995. His paltry $140,000 salary, which was prorated to the 48-game schedule, worked out to about $80,000! After arbitration his income was considerably higher. According to the terms of the NHL Collective Bargaining Agreement, the maximum Brodeur can receive is $850,000.

3.2 **D. Billy Smith**
In 18 NHL seasons, Smith recorded just 22 shutouts, little better than one career SO per season. So it's no surprise that during the veteran Islanders' Vezina year, 1981–82, his 32–9–4 record and 2.97 GAA produced zero

shutouts, an NHL first for a Vezina-winning netminder. Interestingly, Smith's Vezina was the first awarded under a new criterion, the general manager's vote. (All previous winners, back to 1927, won on fewest goals-against—the current measure for the Jennings Trophy.) Perhaps that's one reason why Smith could cop top goalie honours while still being bereft of shutouts. Even so, no other goalie before him who had won the Vezina single-handedly under the old criterion was able to do so without a few shutouts of help.

3.3 B. Arturs Irbe

Irbe, of the San Jose Sharks, became the European with the most NHL games played during the 1995 season, when the Latvian-born, Russian-trained goalie played 38 matches to amass 161 career games, enough to move him ahead of Lindbergh's career total of 157 and Hasek's 152. Polish-born Sidorkiewicz played 245 NHL contests (Hartford, Ottawa and New Jersey) between 1987 and 1994, but his formative junior years were in Canada with the OHL's Oshawa Generals.

3.4 B. Ed Giacomin

The first netminder credited with two points in a single game was the Rangers' Ed Giacomin, who in a March 19, 1972, game against the Leafs assisted on goals by Bill Fairbairn and Pete Stemkowski in a 5–3 New York win.

3.5 A. Corey Hirsch

For Swedish hockey fans, the 1994 Olympics symbolized the pinnacle of success. After several frustrating years of silver and bronze medal finishes, Sweden's moment came in dramatic fashion: a final-round shootout that pitted star forward Peter Forsberg against Hirsch. It was over in a second and Sweden had its first Olympic gold medal. Many commemorative items would honour that historic goal, including a Swedish postage stamp that would have depicted the likeness of Hirsch being deked out by Forsberg. But the Canadian netminder said "No way." So Sweden cast their national hero triumphantly scoring on . . . an unidentifiable goalie.

3.6 C. Jim Carey

After winning only three of their first 18 games in 1995, the Capitals, desperate for help, called up Carey from the AHL. Washington proceeded on a 13–2–2 tear. In his first NHL month, March of 1995, Carey was named Player of the Week, Rookie of the Month and Player of the Month. If that kind of start had anything to do with Carey's superstitions, don't expect to see his sister Ellen at any games soon. The bad luck dates back to Carey's high school days in Massachusetts. His sister attended two games all year, and they were the only games he lost. When it happened again with Portland in the AHL, Carey barred her indefinitely. But what really sealed Ellen's fate was the game at Boston Garden. With his bad-luck sister absent, Carey and the Capitals won. It was Washington's first victory at the Garden in a year.

3.7 D. John Davidson

Phil Esposito and Ken Hodge were not the only Rangers to double their single-digit jersey numbers (from No. 7 and No. 8 to No. 77 and No. 88 respectively) after their trade from Boston to New York in 1975–76. Espo thought the idea was so good, he convinced Davidson to wear No. 00 on his back. Although Espo and Hodge's double-digit sweater numbers launched the trend Wayne Gretzky made famous, for Davidson, his double zero look lasted just one forgettable season. He played poorly and the crowds taunted him mercilessly with "00" jeers (jabs like: "Hey Johnny, is that your I.Q.?"). "I didn't enjoy it. I did it for Phil," recalls Davidson.

3.8 C. Rob Ramage

Smith became the first NHL goaltender to receive credit for a goal after an errant pass by Ramage ended up in his own net. Here's how the November 28, 1979, play unfolded: On a delayed penalty call to the Islanders, the puck bounced into the corner after a Smith save. Ramage picked it up and blindly passed it back to an unmanned point position. The puck slid the length of the ice and into the Rockies' empty net (empty because of the sixth Colorado attacker). Since Smith was the last Islander to touch the puck, he was credited with the goal. Despite the Smith-Ramage goal, the Rockies beat New York 7–4, the first ever Colorado victory against the Islanders.

3.9 D. 58

It wasn't the most shots a goalie faced in a game, but McAuley, who saw Detroit red all night, still produced an NHL record, or, more precisely, *allowed* the Red Wings a record: most consecutive goals by one team in one game (15). The rookie Ranger goalie was blitzed with 58 shots, but stopped 43—a great performance under most circumstances. If McAuley's pals on defense disappeared, his New York offense (an oxy-moron) shouldn't have bothered dressing. They direct-ed only nine shots on Detroit goalie Connie Dion in the entire game. Counting assists, every Red Wing player figured in the scoring except Dion and defenseman Cully Simon. Detroit players accounted for 35 individ-ual points.

3.10 C. Between 20 and 30
Because it's so difficult to predict how well junior goalies will develop, NHL team scouts and general man-agers rarely select netminders early; they wait until the later rounds for a backstopper. Among the 540 first-rounders chosen between 1969 and 1995, only four per cent, or 23, were goalies, a record five being selected in 1994 alone.

3.11 B. 1912–13 Sweet Caporal
When tobacco manufacturers began producing hockey cards in 1909–10, they sold them on their cigarette packs—literally. The hockey card was one side of the cardboard pack, which usually contained four Sweet Caporal cigarettes for a nickel. Today, the 1½-by-2½-inch black-and-white photos of hockey legends, such as Art Ross, Cyclone Taylor and Lester Patrick, are valued at U.S.$11,000 for a set of 50 in mint condition. Roy is a serious collector with hundreds of sets, but the 1912–13 Sweet Caporal issue is his favourite.

3.12 D. More than 33,000 minutes
Hall played 33,135 minutes in 552 regular-season and playoff games for Detroit and Chicago between October 6, 1955, and November 7, 1962. His streak ended during his 552nd game at 10:21 of the first period. Simple mul-tiplication is enough to figure out choice D. Here's the math: 551 complete games times 60 minutes/game equals 33,060 minutes. Add that figure to Hall's 552nd

game minutes (10:21) and his playoff overtime minutes (65:12) and the exact total is 33,135 minutes and 33 seconds of consecutive hockey.

3.13 A. The Canadiens' Bill Durnan

Flush from victory after whipping a young Toronto team 6–0 in game one of the finals, a confident Durnan quipped to reporters: "How did these guys ever make the playoffs?" Coach Hap Day flashed Durnan's reckless remarks around Toronto's dressing room and the return fire stunned Montreal. The Habs went down in four of the next five games to surrender to the youngest Stanley Cup winners ever. The lesson learned: Never underestimate your rivals, especially out loud.

3.14 C. Buffalo's Dominik Hasek

Not since Parent's 1.89 GAA in 1973–74 had an NHL goalie allowed fewer than two goals per game over a season. Hasek managed the feat in 1993–94, when the Czech netminder yielded just 109 goals in 58 games for a 1.95 GAA, and recorded a league-leading seven shutouts for the Sabres.

GAME 3

THE 20-YEAR MEN

The NHL list of 20-year players is an exclusive one. To reach that milestone 20th season requires a combination of good health and great hockey skills. Even players such as Phil Esposito and Dave Keon, who had the legs and held their competitive edge, still missed the 20-year mark by two seasons.

Interestingly, most 20-year men came from the six-team era, between 1942 and 1967. Why? Perhaps, in some cases, NHL expansion in 1967 extended the careers of Original Six players, but, also, old schedules were shorter and travel was frequently less demanding. Attitude may be another reason. The Original Six player had fewer options available; he had to work to maintain his position on one of only six clubs or face a career in the minors.

The 23 20-year men listed below appear in the puzzle, horizontally, vertically or backwards. Some are easily found, like Gordie HOWE, the all-time seasons-played leader; others require a more careful search. After you've circled all 23 names, read the remaining letters in descending order to spell the NHL's first 20-year man and his team. Our mystery player is posing in the puzzle sketch.

(Solutions are on page 115)

ARMSTRONG	HORTON	NESTERENKO	SAWCHUK
BÉLIVEAU	HOWE	PRENTICE	STANLEY
BUCYK	HOWELL	PRONOVOST	STEWART
DELVECCHIO	KELLY	RATELLE	ULLMAN
GADSBY	MIKITA	RICHARD	WORSLEY
HARVEY	MOHNS	ROBINSON	

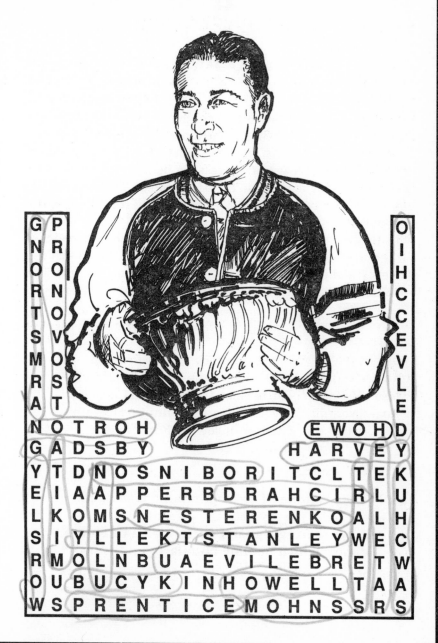

Dit Clapper Boston Bruins

```
G P                              O I
N R                              I H
O O                              H C
R N                              C C
T O                              C E
S V                              E V
M O                              V L
R S                              L E
A T                              E
N O T R O H                      E W O H  D
G A D S B Y                      H A R V E Y
Y T D N O S N I B O R I T C L T E K
E I A A P P E R B D R A H C I R L U
L K O M S N E S T E R E N K O A L H
S I Y L L E K T S T A N L E Y W E C
R M O L N B U A E V I L E B R E T W
O U B U C Y K I N H O W E L L T A A
W S P R E N T I C E M O H N S S R S
```

4

WHO AM I?

Who was Canada's "athlete of the half-century"? He was a four-sport player, competing at the top levels in football, boxing, lacrosse and hockey. As an NHL All-Star defenseman, he captured two Stanley Cups in 12 seasons before retiring in 1937. Despite his wide acclaim as the best athlete Canada ever produced, he was only inducted posthumously into the Hockey Hall of Fame in 1994. *Who is he?*

In this chapter we change the multiple-choice format of earlier chapters and supply all 15 correct answers. Match the players listed below with their "Who am I?" descriptions. The remaining 16th name is Canada's athlete of the half-century.

(Answers are on page 44)

Joe Sakic	John Ogrodnick	Guy Charron
Moe Mantha	Bill Goldsworthy	Dominik Hasek
Jason Herter	Patrik Sundstrom	Lionel Conacher
Roger Neilson	Michel Plasse	Bronco Horvath
Joe Cirella	Gump Worsley	Réal Cloutier
	Bobby/Brett Hull	

4.1 **They call me "The Dominator."** *Who am I?*

4.2 **After scoring a goal, I performed a celebratory dance, which became popularly known as "The Goldy Shuffle."** *Who am I?*

4.3 We are the only father and son duo to win the Hart Trophy as league MVP in NHL history. *Who are we?*

4.4 I hold the NHL record for most teams coached: six and counting! *Who am I?*

4.5 I've played the most regular-season games without a single post-season appearance. *Who am I?*

4.6 I had a good news bad news kind of year in 1989–90, scoring +100 points for my last-place team. *Who am I?*

4.7 My claim to NHL fame is twofold. In 1987, the Canucks traded me to the Devils for Kirk McLean and Greg Adams. Eight months later, with New Jersey, I became the first NHLer to score eight points in a playoff game. *Who am I?*

4.8 I was the only player from the six-team era, between 1942 to 1967, to be signed by all six teams. *Who am I?*

4.9 During my Red Wing days in the 1980s, they called me "Johnny O." *Who am I?*

4.10 I have the unfortunate distinction of being the highest drafted player to go the longest without playing a single NHL game. *Who am I?*

4.11 I was the first goalie in professional hockey to shoot and score a goal, even before Ron Hextall did it in the NHL. *Who am I?*

4.12 I began my hockey career in Winnipeg, where I was traded to Pittsburgh as a future consideration for a Norris Trophy winner (top defenseman), only to be later traded to Edmonton for another Norris winner. *Who am I?*

4.13 In my first NHL game I scored my first—and my team's first—hat trick. It happened in 1979 (the year of the NHL-WHA merger). *Who am I?*

4.14 I hold the dubious honour of surrendering a number of milestone goals, including both Gordie Howe's 500th and Bobby Orr's first. *Who am I?*

4.15 I am the last Colorado Rockie to play in the NHL. *Who am I?*

WHO AM I?
Answers

4.1 "The Dominator." It's a title richly deserved for Buffalo's **Dominik Hasek**. After recording the best goals-against average (1.95) of the past 20 seasons in 1993–94, Hasek furthered his reputation as one of the league's most dominant netminders in 1995's 48-game schedule with a league-low 2.11 GAA. For his sterling two-year effort, the Czechoslovakian copped back-to-back Vezina and Jennings Trophies while inking a three-year $8-million contract. You might say being stingy in the nets has made the Dominator a wealthy man.

4.2   While in Minnesota, **Bill Goldsworthy** developed his own post-goal choreography called "The Goldy Shuffle." Never construed as deft footwork, the on-ice jig became a fan favourite, with everyone expecting the simple shuffle and pump motion after a Goldsworthy goal.

4.3   Since the Hart was first presented in 1924, **Bobby and Brett Hull** have been the only father-son MVP winners. Bobby collected his back-to-back Hart honours with Chicago in 1965 and 1966; a quarter-century later, Brett, in 1991, earned his with St. Louis.

4.4   **Roger Neilson** has been coaching almost continuously since 1977, when he started his NHL career with Toronto (160 games). After being fired (twice) by Leaf boss Harold Ballard, Neilson was hired by Scotty Bowman's Sabres (106 games), followed by stints with Vancouver (133 games, including taking the Canucks to the Cup finals in 1982), Los Angeles (28 games), New York (280 games) and Florida (132 games). Entering 1995–96, Neilson was looking for his seventh head coaching assignment.

4.5   **Guy Charron** played in 734 regular-season games (221-309-530) from 1969 to 1981 without once reaching the playoffs. His 12-season NHL career took him to four different clubs, including five games with the 1969-70 Montreal Canadiens, the only Habs team to miss the playoffs between 1948 and 1995.

4.6   The best slant on Quebec's abysmal last-place finish (12–6–7) in 1989–90 was the performance of star-in-waiting **Joe Sakic**, who, in only his second NHL year, netted 39 goals and 102 points while his Nordiques finished 21st overall, an astounding 33 points behind 20th-place Vancouver. Lost in a season gone for naught,

Sakic's one-man show produced another ignominious twist: Sakic and Quebec were the first 100-point player/last-place team tandem in NHL history.

4.7 In exchange for goalie McLean and centre Adams, the Devils picked up Swedish sniper **Patrik Sundstrom**, who, on April 22, 1988, scored an unprecedented eight playoff points (3G–5P) in a 10–4 New Jersey win over the Capitals. Sundstrom's playoff record has only been equalled by Mario Lemieux.

4.8 **Bronco Horvath** is the only NHLer to have signed with all Original Six teams. Horvath went to Detroit in 1955, but was dealt to the Rangers before playing in any Wing games. After that, Horvath spent time in Montreal, Boston (his best years), Chicago and Toronto, ending his nine-year NHL career in Minnesota during the NHL's first expansion year, 1967-68.

4.9 During the pre-Jacques Demers days of the 1980s, the cellar-dwelling Red Wings struggled along without much offensive punch, except for the play of Steve Yzerman and the man they called "Johnny O." **John Ogrodnick** mounted two 40-goal seasons (41 goals in 1982–83 and 42 in 1983–84) before his 105-point year, 1984–85. It was Johnny O's career year. He popped 55 goals, good enough for seventh place in the NHL scoring race and a berth on the first All-Star team of 1985. The Wings finished third in the Norris Division and bowed out 3–0 to Chicago in the first round, wasting Ogrodnick's stellar year.

4.10 While first-rounders usually get plenty of opportunities to prove themselves with the big club, that hasn't been the story for defenseman Jason Herter, the Canucks' first choice and eighth overall pick of 1989. As of 1995, Herter had not a single NHL game to his credit. He played in North Dakota (WCHA), Milwaukee (IHL) and

Hamilton (AHL) for four years before being signed as a free agent by Dallas in 1993. The Stars' signing changed little and Herter's next stop was Kalamazoo (IHL), where he is still waiting for his NHL chance.

4.11 Ron Hextall may be the NHL's first goalie to actually shoot and score a goal (December 8, 1987), but **Michel Plasse** was the first in professional hockey. Plasse, whose 11-year NHL career took him to six teams between 1970 and 1982, scored hockey's first "goalie goal" on February 21, 1971, while playing as a rookie with the Kansas City Blues of the Central Hockey League. In the final 44 seconds, with a sixth attacker on the ice for Oklahoma City, Plasse cleared the puck, unintentionally shooting it into the empty Blazers net for the 3–1 win. The historic goal was witnessed by only 850 fans. A blizzard, which delayed the game for 90 minutes, kept the crowds away.

4.12 Twelve-year NHL veteran defenseman **Moe Mantha**, from Lakewood, Ohio, was twice dealt for Norris winners: first in 1984 for Pittsburgh's Randy Carlyle (1981 Norris), and three years later to Edmonton for Paul Coffey (1985 and 1986 Norrises).

4.13 Only months after winning the WHA's final scoring title, the Nordiques' **Réal Cloutier** pumped three goals in his—and Quebec's—first NHL game on October 10, 1979. Unfortunately, the Nords lost their home-opener to Atlanta 5-3, but Cloutier tied a 36-year-old league record for most goals in a first game, established by the Canadiens' Alex Smart in 1943.

4.14 Let's face it, after 932 regular-season and playoff games in 21 NHL seasons, a few historic goals are bound to slip between the pipes. Among the 2,624 career goals **Gump Worsley** gave up in more than 54,000 minutes of hockey, a few are notable, including Howe's 500th and Orr's first. But the Gumper also surrendered Maurice Richard's 600th (regular-season and playoff total); Bobby Hull's first 50th in 1962; Howe's 544th (equalling him with Richard for most career goals) and 600th; and Bernie Geoffrion's five-goal game in 1955. What would a goalie be without a few stories to tell?

4.15 **Joe Cirella**, who began his NHL career with the Rockies in Colorado's last season, 1981–82, was still playing with the Florida Panthers in 1995, outlasting fellow Rockie Rob Ramage, who retired in 1993-94.

GAME 4

WAYNE GRETZKY—YEAR BY YEAR

Every year between 1979 and 1994 Wayne Gretzky achieved a personal or NHL milestone. In the spaces below, fill in the years, from 1979 to 1994, when the Great One accomplished his feats.

(Solutions are on page 116)

1. _____ The year Gretz scored his first NHL goal.
2. _____ The year Gretz passed Phil Esposito's career total of 717 goals.
3. _____ The year Gretz was traded to Los Angeles.
4. _____ The year Gretz set the NHL record for most points in one season, including playoffs, with his 255th point.
5. _____ The year Gretz popped his 50th goal in 39 games.
6. _____ The year Gretz played his fewest games, recorded his fewest totals and won no NHL awards (65 points in 45 games).
7. _____ The year Gretz surpassed Mike Bossy's NHL record for the 500 fastest goals.
8. _____ The year Gretz logged his highest penalty-minute totals: 59 minutes.
9. _____ The year Gretz passed Gordie Howe's career-goal total to set an NHL record: 802 goals.
10. _____ The year Gretz established the all-time league scoring record with his 1,851st point.
11. _____ The year Gretz won his first NHL scoring title as a Los Angeles King.
12. _____ The year Gretz set the NHL's highest single-season goal mark with his 92nd goal.
13. _____ The year Gretz won his seventh-in-a-row scoring title.
14. _____ The year Gretz recorded his 13th straight 100-point season.
15. _____ The year Gretz scored in his NHL-record 51st consecutive game.
16. _____ The year Gretz won his first Lady Byng Trophy as most gentlemanly player.

5

THE OFFENSIVE DEFENSEMEN

It's been said (with some levity) that Paul Coffey only *really* started playing defense under Scotty Bowman in Detroit. But the fact is, Bowman built an offensive system for his 1995 Stanley Cup finalists around the skating skills of Coffey. If Coffey, at left defense, ever got caught out of position after a scoring sortie into the opponent's zone, the left-winger stayed back to cover for him. It's a classic example of Bowman utilizing his best players' talents to optimum advantage. But Coffey rarely got caught, registering a team-leading 58 points and a plus-18 rating in 1995, a tribute as much to Bowman's system as to Coffey's all-round abilities, both on the blueline *and* in leading the rush. In this chapter, we champion the offensive strengths of some of the NHL's best defensemen (and a few others worth remembering).

(Answers are on page 54)

5.1 **Who was the youngest defenseman in NHL history to score 30 goals in a season?**
A. Bobby Orr
B. Paul Coffey
C. Phil Housley
D. Denis Potvin

5.2 **After Bobby Orr, who was the next rearguard to score 30 goals in a season?**
A. Larry Robinson
B. Paul Coffey
C. Denis Potvin
D. Doug Wilson

5.3 Which defenseman's record for most goals in a rookie season did Brian Leetch break in 1988–89?
A. Phil Housley's
B. Reed Larson's
C. Barry Beck's
D. Gary Suter's

5.4 How many of Phil Housley's 77 points in 1983–84 were scored as a defenseman (rather than when he played as a forward that season)?
A. 34 of 77 points
B. 44 of 77 points
C. 54 of 77 points
D. 64 of 77 points

5.5 Who was the last defenseman to win the Hart Trophy as league MVP?
A. Bobby Orr
B. Denis Potvin
C. Rod Langway
D. Ray Bourque

5.6 With which team did Paul Coffey score his 300th NHL goal?
A. The Edmonton Oilers
B. The Pittsburgh Penguins
C. The Los Angeles Kings
D. The Detroit Red Wings

5.7 How many pairs of gloves does Boston's Ray Bourque sweat through in one game of hockey?
A. Three
B. Four
C. Five
D. Six

5.8 Which D-man failed to reach 40 goals in a season by just one goal?
A. Kevin Hatcher
B. Ray Bourque
C. Doug Wilson
D. Denis Potvin

5.9 Who is the only defenseman, other than the Rangers' Sergei Zubov, to lead a first-place team (overall) in scoring?
A. The Bruins' Bobby Orr
B. The Islanders' Denis Potvin
C. The Blackhawks' Pierre Pilote
D. The Red Wings' Paul Coffey

5.10 Who was the first blueliner to score 1,000 career points?
A. Ray Bourque
B. Bobby Orr
C. Denis Potvin
D. Brad Park

5.11 Entering the 1995–96 season, how many defensemen had scored more career points than Bobby Orr's 915 points?
A. One, Denis Potvin
B. Three
C. Five
D. Seven

5.12 Which veteran defenseman took six seasons to score his first goal; a goal that was the first in the Buffalo Sabres' history?
A. Jim Watson
B. Jean-Guy Talbot
C. Doug Barrie
D. Al Hamilton

5.13 **Who was the first rearguard to break one of Bobby Orr's NHL scoring records?**
A. Tom Bladon
B. Ian Turnbull
C. Paul Coffey
D. Ron Stackhouse

5.14 **Who was the first blueliner to win the Conn Smythe Trophy as playoff MVP?**
A. Montreal's Larry Robinson
B. Boston's Bobby Orr
C. Montreal's Serge Savard
D. Toronto's Tim Horton

5.15 **Who was the first defenseman in NHL history to score 300 career goals?**
A. Ray Bourque
B. Denis Potvin
C. Bobby Orr
D. Paul Coffey

5.16 **If the NHL record for the most shorthanded goals in one season is 13 (by a forward), what is the record by a defenseman?**
A. Seven shorthanded goals
B. Nine shorthanded goals
C. 11 shorthanded goals
D. 13 shorthanded goals

5.17 **How many more points does Bobby Orr have than Paul Coffey in the NHL record for most regular-season points by a rearguard?**
A. One point
B. Four points
C. Seven points
D. 10 points

THE OFFENSIVE DEFENSEMEN
Answers

5.1 A. Bobby Orr

When Orr scored 33 goals in 1969–70, it was difficult to choose the more impressive feat: recording the NHL's first 30-goal season by a rearguard, or his age—just 22. After three respectable Bruin years (41, 31 and 64 points) between 1966 and 1969, Orr finally unleashed the offensive force that would dominate individual point scoring for five NHL seasons and, ultimately, change the defensive position forever. No one had ever controlled an up-ice rush like Orr. In that 1969–70 season, his 120 points led all NHL players, another NHL first for a defenseman.

5.2 C. Denis Potvin

After Orr registered the NHL's first (of five) +30-goal seasons (33 goals in 1969–70) by a defenseman, Potvin scored 31 goals in 1975–76, becoming the NHL's second +30-goal D-man.

THE NHL'S FIRST 30-GOAL DEFENSEMEN						
Year	Player	Team	GP	G	A	PTS.
1969–70	B. Orr	Bos	76	33	87	120
1970–71	B. Orr	Bos	78	37	102	139
1971–72	B. Orr	Bos	76	37	80	117
1973–74	B. Orr	Bos	74	32	90	122
1974–75	B. Orr	Bos	80	46	89	135
1975–76	D. Potvin	NYI	78	31	67	98
1977–78	D. Potvin	NYI	80	30	64	94
1978–79	D. Potvin	NYI	73	31	70	101
1981–82	D. Wilson	Chi	76	39	46	85
1983–84	P. Coffey	Edm	80	40	86	126
1983–84	R. Bourque	Bos	78	31	65	96
1983–84	P. Housley*	Buf	75	31	46	77
* *Also played as a forward.*						

5.3 C. Barry Beck's

Selected as the second junior overall by Colorado in 1977, Beck tore out of the starting blocks and fired 22 tallies to establish a new NHL rookie goal-scoring mark for defensemen—a record that went unequalled until Leetch's 23-goal surge in 1988–89. The six- foot-three, 215-pound Beck took runner-up honours in Calder Trophy voting and compiled 60 points for the 1977–78 Rockies, a fourth-year expansion team, which finished second in the old Smythe Division. Interestingly, besides Beck, two other defensemen during 1977–78 broke the old rookie goal-scoring record of 17 goals, Minnesota's Brad Maxwell (18) and Detroit's Reed Larson (19).

5.4 D. 64 of 77 points

Former Buffalo general manager Scotty Bowman demonstrated his hockey genius again, this time by drafting rearguard Housley direct from high school in 1982. The Sabre's first choice, and sixth overall NHL pick, turned in a runner-up Rookie of the Year performance (19–47–66) before following in his second season, 1983–84, with 31 goals and 46 assists for 77 points. Moving between centre and defense, Housley picked up 24 of 31 goals and 40 of 46 assists as a blueliner; or 64 of 77 points. Housley was only 20.

5.5 A. Bobby Orr

The last defenseman to win the league MVP award is Orr, who snagged his third and final Hart in 1972 with a 37–80–117 record. Bourque (1987, 1990), Potvin (1976) and Langway (1984) all finished as runners-up in MVP balloting.

5.6   B. The Pittsburgh Penguins

No rearguard has ever matched Coffey's monstrous offensive records. As one of the NHL's most gifted skaters, Coffey racked up career points faster than many forwards, scoring his 300th goal while playing for Pittsburgh on January 5, 1991. It was his 777th game and 11th NHL season.

5.7   D. Six

Bourque, who plays in excess of 30 minutes per game with the Bruins, sweats through six pairs of gloves in a single game. During intermission the gloves are tossed in a dryer.

5.8   C. Doug Wilson

The former Blackhawk rearguard staged his Norris Trophy-winning season in 1981–82, scoring 85 points and 39 goals, just one tally shy of the coveted 40-goal plateau, a milestone reached only by Bobby Orr and Paul Coffey. Of some consolation, Wilson was only the third defenseman in NHL history to score 30 goals in a season.

5.9   D. The Red Wings' Paul Coffey

No D-man had ever led a first overall team in scoring until 1993–94, when Zubov racked up 89 points for first-place New York. Curiously, it happened again the next year to the regular-season champion Red Wings, who finished 1995's 48-game sked with 15-year veteran rearguard Coffey (14–44–58) atop their team point parade. Coffey's 58 points bested all Wings, including star forwards Sergei Fedorov (50), Dino Ciccarelli (43), Keith Primeau (42), Ray Sheppard (40) and Steve Yzerman (38). Bobby Orr's first scoring championship in 1969–70 almost qualified him as the answer here, but Orr's Bruins only tied the Blackhawks for most points (99) in the standings that season. Chicago was awarded first because they won five more games than Boston.

5.10 C. Denis Potvin

The eventful game occurred on April 4, 1987, when Potvin achieved an NHL first for defensemen: he scored 1,000 points. The milestone 1,000th came after a Mikko Makela shot ricocheted off Potvin's arm and sailed past Sabre goalie Jacques Cloutier into the Buffalo net. Potvin recorded 290 goals and 710 assists to reach point number 1,000.

5.11 C. Five

Larry Murphy was the fifth NHL blueliner to surpass Orr's career points record.

THE NHL'S LEADING POINT-SCORING D-MEN				
Player	GP	G	A	PTS
Paul Coffey*	1078	358	978	1336
Ray Bourque*	1146	323	908	1231
Denis Potvin	1060	310	742	1052
Larry Robinson	1384	208	750	958
Larry Murphy*	1152	233	712	945
Bobby Orr	657	270	645	915
Phil Housley*	909	257	625	882
Active/stats current to 1995.				

5.12 A. Jim Watson

The first Sabre goal in franchise history was scored by Watson at 5:01 of the second period in a 2–1 win over Pittsburgh on October 10, 1970. As well as Buffalo's first goal, it was a milestone in Watson's NHL career. Until that point he had gone goal-less in six Detroit seasons (only 77 games). (If you guessed Al Hamilton, you weren't far off. Hamilton, another veteran rearguard, waited four long years to score his first NHL goal, which he also earned as a Sabre in 1970–71.)

5.13   A. Tom Bladon

Except for a few records, such as most assists in one season by a defenseman, many of Orr's 14 rearguard marks have been broken. The first one fell to Philadelphia's Tom Bladon, who, on December 11, 1977, scored eight points (4G–4A) against Cleveland to best Orr's seven-points-in-a-game record, established in November 1973.

5.14   C. Montreal's Serge Savard

In more than 30 years of Conn Smythe winners, only four defensemen on five occasions have been honoured as playoff MVP. Savard holds no league or team playoff records to distinguish his performance in the 1969 post-season, but, as his MVP status indicates, the Canadiens rearguard dominated all players and the play. Savard's outstanding defensive work helped limit opponents to just 26 goals in 14 playoff games. In 1970, Bobby Orr won the first of his two Conn Smythes.

5.15   B. Denis Potvin

Potvin became the NHL's first 300-goal D-man in his final season on January 14, 1987. The milestone goal came against Quebec rookie Ron Tugnutt, who Potvin beat with a wrist shot from the slot in the 8–5 win. Potvin was the 65th player in NHL history to score 300 goals. He did it in his 1,023rd career game. The 15-year Islander capped his remarkable career with 310 goals, 40 more than Orr's total of 270. Coffey netted number 300 in 1990–91 with Pittsburgh; Bourque reached the mark with the Bruins in 1993–94.

5.16   B. Nine shorthanded goals

Paul Coffey's career year for goals was 1985–86, when the former Edmonton rearguard scored an amazing 48 times, nine of them shorthanded, to set the NHL standard for D-men. The shorthanded record for forwards is Mario Lemieux's 13 goals in 1988–89.

5.17 A. One point

Orr holds the regular-season points record for blue-liners by just one point over Coffey, 139 points (37G–102A in 78 games, 1970–71) to 138 points (48G–90A in 79 games, 1985–86).

GAME 5

THE CROSSWORD

(Solutions are on page 116)

ACROSS

2. Goal-scoring Flyer goalie in crossword sketch
7. Hold or _____ against the boards
9. "_____ the attack"
11. "Clutch and _____"
12. No red light, _____ _____ (2 words)
13. _____ Angeles Kings
14. Toronto's _____ Apps
15. Boston's Bobby _____
17. "A _____ share"
19. Penalty box or "sin-_____"
21. Rangers arena (abbr.)
22. Arena sound system (abbr.)
23. _____shakes after playoff series
24. Canadian sports channel
26. Steal or _____ a goal
28. Leaving or "Heading for the _____"
30. Look
31. Rock 'em, sock 'em TV man (2 words)
36. Material for sticks
38. 1980 Kings one-game player, Doug _____
39. Player's union (abbr.)
41. Former Jet/Wing goalie Bob _____
42. Montreal's _____ Joliat
43. American sports network (abbr.)
44. 1955s "The Richard _____"
48. Stick infraction: "He _____ his opponent"
51. One-time Kings goalie Robb _____
52. To total up

DOWN

1. First name of 2 Across goalie
3. Think highly of themselves; "players with big _____"
4. Broken bone photo
5. Old name for goal or game score
6. 1961 Hawk, _____ McDonald
7. Late game tactic: "_____ the goalie"
8. Habs/Bruins Swede, Mats _____
10. D-man award, _____ Trophy
15. Montreal's Bert _____
16. Full name of "Rogie" (2 words)
18. What Denis Savard does: "He dekes or _____ around a player"
19. Penguins goalie, Tom _____
20. "Shoo-_____"
25. _____ Louis Blues
27. An open cut will _____
29. Top goalie award, _____ Trophy
32. Dominik _____
33. Flames/Whalers goalie, Jeff _____
34. Not old
35. Word to describe Béliveau
36. The ref cautioned or _____ the players
37. Edmonton player
38. 1980s Flyers centre, Tim _____
40. Florida goalie, Darren _____
45. Extra period (abbr.)
46. From where the Red Army team hailed (abbr.)
47. Béliveau's nickname, "_____ Gros Bill"
49. TV commercial
50. Goalie's favourite win (abbr.)

6

TRIVIA SNIPERS: YOUR SHOT

In our fourth hockey book, we invited readers to send us their own trivia questions for publication. We picked the best selection and fleshed out the answers with our own research. Thanks to everyone for participating. If you want to join next year's edition of Hockey Trivia's Reader Rebound, fill out the form at the back of the book.

(Answers are on page 65)

6.1 How many goals did the New York Islanders score during their four Stanley Cup final-series rounds (1980, 1981, 1982 and 1983)?

Dean Chernoff
Castlegar, British Columbia

6.2 Which NHLer holds the record for most points scored in a single game?

Joseph Fu
Flushing, New York

6.3 In what statistic did Bob Probert lead the NHL, the same season he scored his personal best of 29 goals?

Andrea Werstine
Highland, Michigan

6.4 What was so unusual about Mario Lemieux's first five-goal game?

Randy Denomme
Kitchener, Ontario

6.5 What extra material was used in the skirts of hockey's first female players?

Jenny Carson
Westfield, New Brunswick

6.6 What is the highest uniform number worn by a goalie?

The Parras family
Torrance, California

6.7 Who is the only Toronto Maple Leaf to win the Conn Smythe Trophy as playoff MVP?

Rajji Vikram
Hastings, New York

6.8 How many American-born players have scored more than 1,000 career points in regular-season play?

Joseph Valenti
Manalapan, New Jersey

6.9 The first player ever drafted by Edmonton also scored the first Oiler NHL goal in team history. Who is he?

Matt Ring
Winnipeg, Manitoba

6.10 What is Mark Messier's favourite charity?

Tara Dawson
Centereach, New York

6.11 What player scored the most goals per game in one season?

Wayne Tracey
Montreal, Quebec

6.12 Who are the only three players in NHL history to record a 30-goal/300-penalty-minute season?

Gretta Paugh
Warren, Ohio

6.13 Which Calgary Flame retired in 1990, only to return in 1995 for a brief six-game stint?

Nik Thorington
Winnipeg, Manitoba

6.14 Which New York Islander holds the NHL record for most points in a single period?

Tom Lener
Mount Kisco, New York

6.15 What was the Montreal street address of Toe Blake's Tavern?

Ryan Olsen
St. Laurent, Quebec

6.16 What was the value of the Stanley Cup when Canada's Governor General, Lord Stanley of Preston, donated it as a championship hockey trophy in 1892?

Chuck Patterson
Belmont, California

6.17 Who was the lowest-drafted player to win the regular-season scoring championship?

Aimee Craze
Alexandria, Virginia

TRIVIA SNIPERS: YOUR SHOT
Answers

6.1 Because of the sheer volume of team and individual records established by the Gretzky-led Oilers during their dynasty years of the 1980s, we tend to overlook the scoring prowess of the Islanders in their glory days. Between 1980 and 1983, the Isles, led by Mike Bossy, Bryan Trottier and Denis Potvin, scored an amazing **87 goals** in just 19 final-round games to capture four Stanley Cups. By comparison, Edmonton's powerhouse needed more games (22) and scored fewer goals (85) to win their four championships.

6.2 Toronto's **Darryl Sittler** holds the NHL record for most points in one game, scoring six goals and four assists for 10 points on February 7, 1976. The 11–4 win over Boston is the only NHL game in which a player recorded a double-digit tally. Sittler's victim was the Bruins' Dave Reese, who, after the blowout, never played another NHL game. Which Boston coach left Reese swinging in the wind? None other than popular hockey commentator Don Cherry, whose back-up goalie that night was Gerry Cheevers. Back in the NHL for only his first game after a three-year WHA stint, Cheevers kept a low profile on the bench to avoid any participation in the nightmare unfolding before him. Cherry obliged the one-time Stanley Cup-winning goalie. The next night, Cheevers, in the Bruins net in Detroit, recorded a shutout.

6.3 While scoring a career-high 29 goals with Detroit in 1987–88, Probert led the league in, what else, **box time**—398 penalty minutes.

6.4 Lemieux's first five-goal game also produced an NHL first. **He scored a goal every possible way**: at even strength, on the power play, shorthanded, on a penalty shot and into an empty net. It happened in an 8–6 win over New Jersey on December 31, 1988.

6.5 Hockey's early female players often used **buckshot** in the hem of their ankle-length skirts. The buckshot weighed down the long linen skirts, preventing them from flying up after an "embarrassing" fall on the ice. By the 1920s, the long skirts were gone, replaced by leggings and bloomers.

6.6 Darren Puppa is the first NHL goalie to follow the trend of high jersey numbers, started essentially by Wayne Gretzky's No. 99 in the late 1970s. Many skaters copied the Great One into the high double digits, but goalies kept to traditional numbers, such as 1, 29 or 30. Puppa wore No. 31 in Buffalo; after his arrival in Tampa Bay in 1993, he picked **No. 93**, to break with tradition and celebrate the year of his move to the Lightning.

6.7 **Dave Keon** is Toronto's only Conn Smythe winner. He captured the playoff NHL award in 1967, the last year the Leafs won the Stanley Cup. Keon, who scored just two points in the Toronto-Montreal final, won the MVP honours based on his defensive performance.

6.8 New York native **Joe Mullen is the only U.S.-born player** to reach the 1,000-point plateau, scoring 1,026 points in 971 games over 15 NHL seasons.

JOE MULLEN'S 1,000-POINT NHL REGISTER						
Seasons	Team	GP	G	A	PTS	PIM
1979/1986	St. Louis	301	151	184	335	45
1986/1990	Calgary	345	190	198	388	95
1990/1995	Pittsburgh	325	146	157	303	97
	Totals*	971	487	539	1026	237

Totals current to 1995.

6.9 **Kevin Lowe** was the first Oiler pick, chosen 21st in the 1979 entry draft. Months later, on October 10, 1979, he scored Edmonton's first NHL goal in the club's initial game, a 4–2 loss to Chicago.

6.10 Messier's favourite charity is the **Tomorrows Children's Fund**, run by the Hackensack Medical Centre in New Jersey. The fund helps kids with cancer and blood disorders. Since Mark began fund-raising in 1993, he has personally raised $275,000 through auctions, sponsorships and the Mark Messier Point Club. For every point he scores, Mark donates $100 to the 20-bed cancer clinic.

6.11 No NHLer has ever matched the phenomenal pace of goal scoring that **Joe Malone** established during the 22-game 1917–18 season, when the Canadiens star scored 44 goals in 20 games for a 2.20 goals-per-game average. While only a small number of players have ever produced one five-goal game in their careers, in that season alone Malone notched a record of three five-goal games. In today's terms, Malone's average would produce a 180-goal season.

6.12 The 30-goal/300-penalty-minute season is an exclusive club. Who could earn 300 minutes of gate time and still produce respectable goal totals? Bob Probert, maybe. But even Probie, with the heaviest fists in the league, never recorded a 30-goal season (29 goals and 398 minutes in 1987–88). We found only three: **Dave Williams, Al Secord and Rick Tocchet.**

THE NHL'S 30-GOAL/300 PIM CLUB						
Season	Player	Team	G	A	Pts	PIM
1980–81	D. Williams	Van	35	27	62	343
1981–82	A. Secord	Chi	44	31	75	303
1987–88	R. Tocchet	Phi	31	33	64	301

6.13 After a 10-season NHL career (161–262–423) and five years of retirement, longtime Flame forward **Jim Peplinski** made a comeback attempt in 1995. But the game had changed too much for Peplinski, who, at age 35, scored just one point in six games.

6.14 **Bryan Trottier** is tied for a number of NHL records, but no one has equalled his six-point spree of the second period on December 23, 1978, when he scored three goals and three assists against the Rangers in a 9–4 Isles victory.

6.15 Little more than a two-minute cab ride from the Montreal Forum, stuck in between a cigar shop and Leader's Bowling Lanes, was the non-descript entrance of Toe Blake's Tavern at **1618 St. Catherine Street West**. In the days before "Women Welcome" establishments, Toe Blake's was a sanctuary for the boys, where they could chin wag until the wee hours over pints of ale and a few cigars. Topics ranged from which Canadiens' dynasty had the best talent or who was better, Gordie or Maurice, to some old Maroons story that became taller with each telling. Blake's tavern was the mecca for hockey philosophers and armchair coaches, a preserve steeped in hockey knowledge second only to the Canadiens coach's office at the Forum. Today, the entire block has been replaced by a mall complex.

6.16 In 1892, Lord Stanley paid a British silversmith 10 guineas, or **Cdn.$48.67,** to produce a simple silver bowl called the Dominion Hockey Challenge Cup. It immediately became known as the Stanley Cup, and soon grew in size as a silver barrel was added (below the bowl) to accommodate the names of each year's champions. Today, the Stanley Cup is the oldest competed-for trophy in North American sport. It is considered priceless.

6.17 There are no spectacularly late picks that fooled everyone and went on to win the NHL's scoring title. In fact, only half of all scoring champs have ever been drafted at all. That's because the NHL draft began in 1983 and much of the top talent during that era had already signed player contracts to NHL-sponsored junior teams. Further, Wayne Gretzky, who dominates the champion's list as a 10-time Art Ross Trophy winner, was never drafted because he had signed a long-term deal with the WHA Oilers before their merger into the NHL in 1979. Excuses aside, the winner is **Bryan Trottier**, chosen 22nd overall in 1974. (Worth mentioning: Brett Hull managed runner-up status to Gretzky in the 1991 scoring race after his 117th selection in 1984's draft).

THE DRAFTING OF NHL SCORING LEADERS

Scoring Champion	Winning Years	Draft Round	Position Overall	Draft Year
B. Trottier	1979	2nd	22nd	1974
J. Jagr	1995	1st	5th	1990
M. Dionne	1980	1st	2nd	1971
M. Lemieux	1988/89 1992/93	1st	1st	1984
G. Lafleur	1976/77/78	1st	1st	1971
W. Gretzky	1981–87 1990/91/94	Never drafted		
B. Orr	1970/75	Never drafted		
P. Esposito	1969/71–74	Never drafted		
S. Mikita	1964/65 1967/68	Never drafted		
B. Hull	1966	Never drafted		

GAME 6

"LET'S SEE IF THEY KICK ME OFF THE ICE!"

When Wayne Gretzky found out that his trademark helmet, the Jofa 235, was considered unsafe by the NHL, he fired back: "I've worn my helmet 17 years and now they're afraid I'm going to get hurt. It's a big issue to them, but I'm going to wear the helmet I always have. Let's see if they kick me off the ice!"

While Gretzky and the league sort out if this is a safety and/or a licensing issue, you can play "What's my Line?" by matching the hockey orators below with their quotes.

(Solutions are on page 117)

Part 1

Brett Hull	Pat Burns	Harold Ballard
Harry Neale	Marcel Aubut	Pat Flatley
	Wendel Clark	

1._____ "Hockey is bilingual."

2._____ "It's a little like wrestling a gorilla; you don't quit when you get tired, you quit when the gorilla gets tired." (On picking a fight with a tough guy.)

3._____ "If people want to see a picture of the Queen, they can go to an art gallery. What the hell, she doesn't pay me. I pay her." (After tearing down the Royal portrait at Maple Leaf Gardens.)

4._____ "Quebec no longer has the means to let its dreams live on."

5._____ "The centre is your support guy. He's busier than a one-legged man in an ass-kicking contest."

6._____ "I'm going to play until the Zamboni comes and scrapes me off the ice."

7._____ "Yep, but I can do it about 60 times a year." (Player's response at a team physical after being asked: "Is that as high as you can raise your arms?")

Part 2

Jamie Baker	Bob Berry	Gilbert Perreault
Jason Arnott	Mike Keane	Barry Melrose
	Mike Keenan	

1._____ "I've got to get him a Goodyear endorsement." (On the amount of shots goalie Curtis Joseph faces each season.)

2._____ "The nice girls, you get their phone numbers and take them for dinners and whatnot. The real cheesy girls who go home with you in a second, those are the type of girls you've got to stay away from."

3._____ "If you want security, I'd get a job at the post office. You're there for life, or until they shoot you."

4._____ "Forecheck, backcheck, paycheck."

5._____ "This wasn't a hockey game. It was a dog fight between a pit bull and a Chihuahua." (After a 1995 Detroit-San Jose playoff game.)

6._____ "Tell him I can't hear a word he said. I've got a Stanley Cup ring in my ear." (Player's response after being told that Al Iafrate didn't like his playing style.)

7._____ "I didn't know you could sit in the penalty box that long." (After a 60-day suspension.)

7

LINE IN THE ICE: THE LOCKOUT

While we all missed the NHL during 1994–95's labour lockout, a few good things came of it. Europe witnessed the league's best courtesy of Wayne Gretzky's seven-game goodwill tour, the NHL Players' Association Four-on-Four Challenge raised $700,000 for charities and, in the absence of NHL hockey, attendance (in most cases) at the minor pro level increased. But the best news was the NHL Collective Bargaining Agreement, which both sides saw as a win-win deal.

(Answers are on page 75)

7.1 **What player's streak was broken because of the NHL lockout in 1994–95?**
A. Mike Gartner's 15 consecutive 30-goal seasons
B. Patrick Roy's nine consecutive 20-win seasons
C. Wayne Gretzky's 14 consecutive All-Star appearances
D. All of the above

7.2 **Who wrote "Bettman sucks" across the front of his helmet during training camp in October 1994?**
A. The Canadiens' Mathieu Schneider
B. The Blues' Brett Hull
C. The Blackhawks' Chris Chelios
D. The Maple Leafs' Doug Gilmour

7.3 Which defenseman was the first NHLer to file an unemployment claim during the lockout?
A. The Kings' Tim Watters
B. The Sharks' Tom Pederson
C. The Stars' Doug Zmolek
D. The Mighty Ducks' Don McSween

7.4 During the European tour of Wayne Gretzky's All-Star team, what player's name was misspelled on his jersey?
A. Paul Coffey—COFFEE
B. Tony Granato—GRANOTO
C. Russ Courtnall—CORTNALL
D. Steve Yzerman—YXERMAN

7.5 Who was the first NHL player to sustain a major injury while playing in Europe during the lockout?
A. Esa Tikkanen
B. Jari Kurri
C. Viktor Kozlov
D. Christian Ruuttu

7.6 What International Hockey League franchise recorded the highest average attendance during the NHL lockout?
A. The Chicago Wolves
B. The Denver Grizzlies
C. The Detroit Vipers
D. The Houston Aeros

7.7 Who threatened: "If I was Gary Bettman, I'd be worried about my family, about my well-being right now."?
A. Chris Chelios
B. Marty McSorley
C. Jeremy Roenick
D. Bob Goodenow

7.8 Who was the first NHLer to publicly state that many players "would vote to accept" an agreement, at a time when negotiations had broken down between the league and the players' association?
A. Mark Messier
B. Pat Verbeek
C. Ray Bourque
D. Stephane Richer

7.9 What city was supposed to host the 1995 NHL All-Star game?
A. St. Louis
B. San Jose
C. Boston
D. Toronto

7.10 In which European country did Doug Gilmour play for a month during the lockout?
A. Germany
B. Sweden
C. Switzerland
D. Czech Republic

7.11 How long was the lockout?
A. 85 days
B. 95 days
C. 105 days
D. 115 days

7.12 **What was the final vote by players to ratify the new NHL Collective Bargaining Agreement?**
A. 367 for—216 against
B. 417 for—166 against
C. 467 for—116 against
D. 517 for—66 against

7.13 **What percentage of a full year's salary did most players lose during the lockout?**
A. 36 per cent
B. 43 per cent
C. 50 per cent
D. 57 per cent

LINE IN THE ICE: THE LOCKOUT
Answers

7.1 **D. All of the above**
There are plenty of asterisks in the NHL record books due to 1995's lockout-shortened 48-game schedule. Not only did Gartner miss his first 30-goal season in 15 years (he scored just 12 goals in 1995), but Roy, who won 17 games in 1995, ended his nine-year reign of 20-win seasons; and Gretzky's record 14 straight All-Star games was halted. A few more broken streaks: Brett Hull's five consecutive 50-goal seasons (29 goals in 1995); Ray Bourque's five straight 80-point seasons (43 points in 1995); and Ron Francis's streak of 13 20-goal seasons. For the first time in a quarter-century of NHL hockey, there were no 100-point or 50-goal scorers, nor any 100-point teams.

7.2   A. The Canadiens' Mathieu Schneider

Schneider's bit of helmet graffiti raised such an uproar, the former Canadiens defenseman apologized to both NHL commissioner Gary Bettman and Canadiens boss Serge Savard. Bettman responded by saying that the lockout was not personal, but business. There was also a promise by the commish to buy Schneider a beer once everything was settled. No word yet on where they sucked back the suds.

7.3   D. The Mighty Ducks' Don McSween

McSween was the first NHL player to file for unemployment benefits during the lockout. After playing much of his career making $30,000 to $50,000 in the minor pro leagues, McSween, who played 32 games for Anaheim in 1993–94, would earn $300,000 in 1995. Under California law, the 30-year-old locked-out hockey "employee" was eligible for a maximum unemployment claim of $230 a week for 26 weeks.

7.4   B. Tony Granato—GRANOTO

The flashy red-and-white uniforms of Wayne Gretzky's 99 All-Stars were covered with sponsorship logos from Coca-Cola and L.A. Gear, but when it came to Granato's name, it was spelled: Granoto, with an "o" instead of an "a." The typo lasted just one game before being corrected.

7.5   C. Viktor Kozlov

On November 27, 1994, Kozlov suffered a fractured left ankle and damage to an interior ankle ligament while playing with the Moscow Dynamo team in Russia. After surgery, six weeks in a cast and rehab, San Jose's 1993 first-round pick (sixth overall) was back with the Sharks, but played only 16 games in 1995's abbreviated season, scoring just two goals. Kozlov, aged 19, was among more than 80 NHLers performing with teams in Europe.

7.6 C. The Detroit Vipers

While most IHL teams averaged about 7,800 fans per game, the I's expansion franchises in Detroit, Chicago, Denver and Houston did the best business during the NHL lockout. Hungry Motor City hockey fans averaged 13,792 watching the first-year Vipers; while the Wolves averaged 11,293; the Grizzlies, 11,264; and the Aeros, 11,057. Although some clubs benefited in the short term, a number of IHL owners felt hockey was better off with the NHL playing because of increased general interest in the game.

7.7   A. Chris Chelios

Bettman, who withstood a lot of heat from players during the lockout, was least amused by Chelios' outburst. His silly and dangerous remarks earned the Chicago D-man a 45-minute appointment in New York at the commissioner's office, after which Chelios was asked to sign a written apology.

7.8   D. Stephane Richer

The first player to break union solidarity and publicly admit "the guys are fed up with losing money" and "the season would start tomorrow" if a vote were held, was Richer, who made the comments during the lockout's darkest days, when stalled talks halted full-scale negotiating between Gary Bettman and Bob Goodenow. Although Goodenow and the union's bargaining committee rebuked Richer, his quotes were seen as "a small crack" in player solidarity. Within four weeks a deal would be struck.

7.9   B. San Jose

The NHL waited until the last moment to decide the outcome of 1995's All-Star game; on December 8, 1994, the bad news was confirmed. Scheduled for January 21, 1995, the 46th Annual NHL All-Star game at San Jose

Arena was cancelled, due to the league's labour dispute. San Jose will be the host city in 1997.

7.10 C. Switzerland

During the NHL labour dispute, Gilmour played nine games for Rapperswil in the B Division of the Swiss League, where the Leafs captain scored two goals and 15 assists for 17 points in his month-long stint. Although many NHLers have played in Switzerland, including Andy Bathgate, Jacques Lemaire and Mats Naslund, Gilmour's visit was the first by an NHL superstar at the peak of his career. Gilmour's take? Just $1,500 a game, which he donated to the NHL Players' Association.

7.11 C. 105 days

The lockout lasted from October 1, 1994 (the first day of the 1994-95 season), to January 13, 1995, when the NHLPA announced that a majority of players had voted to ratify the NHL's new Collective Bargaining Agreement. The 105-day lockout lasted one day longer than the 1995 48-game, 104-day season.

7.12 D. 517 for—66 against

After many long months of negotiating, on January 11, 1995, the players' union executive and the NHL reached an agreement, which was ratified the next day in a secret ballot vote by the membership, 517–66. The six-year deal gave players free agency at age 32 in the first three years of the contract and at age 31 in the final three. The agreement, which expires September 15, 2000, includes no salary caps and no taxation system. Both sides have the right to re-open negotiations in 1997–98.

7.13 B. 43 per cent

Although a few NHL stars had ironclad, no pay-cut contracts with their clubs, most players lost about 43 per cent of their salaries during the lockout. The figures were prorated on the number of games missed (36) from an 84-game schedule.

NUMBER ONE DRAFT PICKS

Listed below are the first names of many of the best number one overall picks since 1969. Once you've figured out the players' last names, find them in the puzzle by reading across, down or diagonally. As with our example of Wendel C-L-A-R-K, connect the name using letters no more than once. Start with the letters printed in heavy type.

(Solutions are on page 117)

Guy _____   Owen _____   Eric _____

Bobby _____   Mario _____   Mats _____

Denis _____   Gord _____   Roman _____

Dale _____   Joe _____   Oleg _____

Alexandre _____   Mike _____   Gilbert _____

Wendel C-L-A-R-K

```
R M A R E   S E I M E
L L R H P U M S U L M
I E I K S N I H X O K
A N D Y O D P T A L D
L U K R I O H W O A U
T S I N T L-C E A N Z
V N E V T A G I R D A
O L U V Y L R C H O K
D F E R E H P K L U N
  R A L M U R N A K
```

8

TEAMS, COACHES
AND SWEATERS

No team has logged more tied games in one season than the 1969–70 Philadelphia Flyers, who, before the reinstatement of five-minute overtimes in 1983, posted a record 24 deadlocks in the 76-game schedule, an average of about one tie every third game.

In this chapter we combine a variety of hockey topics, including questions and anecdotes about team records, famous coaches and player obsessions with jersey numbers.

(Answers are on page 87)

8.1 **What is the most valuable NHL franchise? (And how much is it worth?)**
A. The New York Rangers
B. The Detroit Red Wings
C. The Chicago Blackhawks
D. The Anaheim Mighty Ducks

8.2 **When Teemu Selanne changed his uniform number in his third NHL season with the Winnipeg Jets, he went from what old number to what new number?**
A. From No. 8 to No. 13
B. From No. 10 to No. 13
C. From No. 13 to No. 10
D. From No. 13 to No. 8

8.3 Which Canadian arena celebrates the opening of each NHL season with the playing of bagpipes?
A. Maple Leaf Gardens in Toronto
B. Northlands Coliseum in Edmonton
C. Winnipeg Arena
D. Civic Centre in Ottawa

8.4 Which team was Scotty Bowman coaching when he reached his 900-win milestone?
A. The Montreal Canadiens
B. The Buffalo Sabres
C. The Detroit Red Wings
D. The Pittsburgh Penguins

8.5 How far away is the Boston Bruins' new arena, the Fleet Center, from Boston Garden, their original home rink?
A. Nine inches
B. Nine feet
C. Nine city blocks
D. Nine miles

8.6 How long did it take the Ottawa Senators to register their first shutout in franchise history?
A. One game
B. Half a season—42 games
C. One 84-game season
D. More than two 84-game seasons

8.7 What International Hockey League club had its coach suspended for attacking an opposing team's mascot in the stands during a 1995 game? (And name the unfortunate mascot.)
A. The Las Vegas Thunder
B. The Cincinnati Cyclones
C. The Detroit Vipers
D. The Peoria Rivermen

8.8 **Which player *never* wore No. 99 on his sweater?**
A. Wilf Paiement
B. Wayne Gretzky
C. Brian Lawton
D. Rick Dudley

8.9 **As of 1995, how many NHL teams broadcast their games in Spanish?**
A. One team
B. Two teams
C. Three teams
D. Four teams

8.10 **Name the only other team Al Arbour has coached besides the New York Islanders.**
A. The Detroit Red Wings
B. The Chicago Blackhawks
C. The Toronto Maple Leafs
D. The St. Louis Blues

8.11 **In what year did the U.S. Olympic hockey team feature The Diaper Line?**
A. 1980
B. 1984
C. 1992
D. 1994

8.12 **Whose idea was it to form the Eric Lindros-John LeClair-Mikael Renberg line?**
A. Flyer general manager Bobby Clarke
B. Flyer head coach Terry Murray
C. Centre Eric Lindros
D. Flyer assistant coach Keith Acton

8.13 What NHL team was the first to score on two penalty shots in one game?

A. The New York Rangers
B. The Edmonton Oilers
C. The Vancouver Canucks
D. The Detroit Red Wings

8.14 Which NHL club was the first to produce four 100-point scorers in one season?

A. The Boston Bruins
B. The St. Louis Blues
C. The Edmonton Oilers
D. The Montreal Canadiens

8.15 On what NHL team did Bernie Nicholls *not* wear No. 9 on his jersey?

A. The Los Angeles Kings
B. The Chicago Blackhawks
C. The New Jersey Devils
D. The New York Rangers

8.16 What team holds the NHL record for the longest undefeated streak from the start of a season?

A. The 1943–44 Montreal Canadiens
B. The 1972–73 Montreal Canadiens
C. The 1984–85 Edmonton Oilers
D. The 1995 Pittsburgh Penguins

8.17 How many Ottawa Senators captains were there in the team's first two seasons?

A. Two
B. Three
C. Four
D. Five

8.18 What was the team record of the Philadelphia Flyers after forming The Legion of Doom line by acquiring John LeClair from Montreal on February 9, 1995?
A. 19–16–3
B. 22–13–3
C. 25–10–3
D. 28–7–3

8.19 Who owns the No. 99 jersey Wayne Gretzky wore when he scored his 801st goal, tying Gordie Howe's all-time scoring record?
A. Gretzky's close friend and agent, Mike Barnett
B. Gretzky's father, Walter Gretzky
C. Gretzky himself
D. The Hockey Hall of Fame

8.20 When was the last time a first-place team selected first overall in the following year's NHL draft? And name the team.
A. It's never happened.
B. 1971, the Montreal Canadiens
C. 1975, the Philadelphia Flyers
D. 1982, the Boston Bruins.

8.21 What is the fastest time in which one team has scored five goals?
A. Less than three minutes
B. Between three and four minutes
C. Between four and five minutes
D. More than five minutes

8.22 What NHL team featured The Crash Line in 1995?
A. The Toronto Maple Leafs
B. The Tampa Bay Lightning
C. The Dallas Stars
D. The New Jersey Devils

8.23 What did former Ranger general manager Phil Esposito give up to acquire coach Michel Bergeron in 1987?

A. Bergeron was hired without compensation to Quebec
B. Bergeron for future considerations
C. Bergeron for cash
D. Bergeron for cash and a New York first-round draft pick

8.24 When Joe Juneau first joined Boston, he asked for a certain uniform number but was turned down by the player who had previously worn it. Who was the player and what number did Juneau want?

A. Bobby Orr's No. 4
B. Phil Esposito's No. 7
C. Johnny Bucyk's No. 9
D. Milt Schmidt's No. 15

8.25 Which NHL team was first to average 20,000 fans per home game in a single season?

A. The St. Louis Blues
B. The Detroit Red Wings
C. The Calgary Flames
D. The Chicago Blackhawks

8.26 In which international hockey series did two teams first exchange jerseys on ice after the winning goal was scored?

A. The Summit Series in 1972
B. The Canada Cup of 1976
C. The Challenge Cup of 1979
D. The Canada Cup of 1981

TEAMS, COACHES AND SWEATERS
Answers

8.1   **B. The Detroit Red Wings**
The Red Wings are the NHL's most valuable franchise, worth $124 million according to *Financial World* magazine. Despite a $20-million jump in value between 1994 and 1995, Detroit still ranks only 47th among all major sports teams. The Dallas Cowboys rate the highest value at $238 million. The next-richest hockey clubs are the Mighty Ducks and the Rangers, each worth $108 million; the Winnipeg Jets are the lowest at $35 million. The main reason cited for increased team values is new sports facilities, such as Detroit's Joe Louis Arena and Arrowhead Pond of Anaheim.

8.2   **D. From No. 13 to No. 8**
In 1995, Selanne switched uniform numbers, giving up his Jets No. 13, which he used for two seasons, to wear No. 8, his jersey number with Jokerit in his native Finland. Randy Carlyle wore No. 8. in Selanne's first NHL season. After the longtime Jet retired in 1993, Selanne waited a season out of respect before making the request.

8.3   **A. Maple Leaf Gardens in Toronto**
Playing the bagpipes has remained a Toronto tradition since the first game at Maple Leaf Gardens on November 12, 1931, when 13,542 spectators watched the 48th Highlanders march onto the ice playing "Happy Days Are Here Again" to christen the Leafs' new home. The bagpipe custom stuck. Today, before each season home opener, the patriotic "The Maple Leaf Forever" wails through the Gardens' hallowed halls, a reminder of the Leafs' rich hockey heritage and a welcome to fans.

8.4 C. The Detroit Red Wings

Bowman coached his 900th win on March 25, 1995, when his Wings downed the Canucks 2–1 before a crowd of 16,083 at the Pacific Coliseum in Vancouver. Sergei Fedorov scored one goal and assisted on another, while goalie Mike Vernon stopped 24 of 25 shots for Detroit, which won its 20th season game.

SCOTTY BOWMAN'S NHL COACHING REGISTER

Team	Games	Wins	Losses	Ties	Cups	Seasons
St. Louis	238	110	83	45	0	1967–71
Montreal	634	419	110	105	5	1971–79
Buffalo	404	210	134	60	0	1979–87
Pittsburgh	164	95	53	16	1	1991–93
Detroit	132	79	41	12	0	1993–
Totals*	1572	913	421	238	6	

* Totals current to 1995.

8.5 A. Nine inches

Built almost wall-upon-wall, the Bruins' new state-of-the-art sports palace, the Fleet Center, is exactly nine inches from Boston Garden.

8.6 D. More than two 84-game seasons

After two seasons and nine games, the Senators finally iced their franchise's first shutout on February 6, 1995. They outhit and outhustled the Flyers throughout the game, winning 3–0 on goals by Alexandre Daigle, Alexei Yashin and Troy Murray. The big key was Ottawa goalie Don Beaupre who played brilliantly, stopping 34 shots before 9,267 fans. Ironically, it was the Civic Centre's smallest crowd since Ottawa joined the NHL in 1992.

8.7   B. The Cincinnati Cyclones

Fights occur between opposing players; between opposing coaches; between coaches and referees; and even between coaches, players and fans. But no head coach had ever taken down a mascot. But this is hockey, where the truly bizarre happens. On February 4, 1995, the usually even-tempered Don Jackson, coach of the Cyclones, completely lost it after the Atlanta Knights' mascot "Sir Slap Shot" banged the glass partition separating the fans from the Cincinnati players. Jackson, leaning against the glass at the time, was knocked into his players. Seconds later, the Cyclones bench boss climbed over the glass divider and began pummelling Sir Slap Shot, to the consternation of many fans. The IHL suspended Jackson for 10 games and fined him $1,000, the same fine levied against Atlanta (because of their mascot's conduct). The Knights won 7–2.

8.8   C. Brian Lawton

Gretzky's No. 99 is not the only double-digit nine in NHL history. In fact, almost a half-century earlier, in 1934–35, three different Canadiens players donned 99s, none making any obvious impact. In modern times, a few other 99s sprouted up around the league, perhaps in the hope of capturing the Gretzky magic: Toronto's Wilf Paiement in 1979–80; and a year later, Winnipeg sported Rick Dudley in a Jets No. 99 uniform. First overall draft pick Brian Lawton, wanting some of the magic without too much of the comparison, chose No. 98 in his 1983–84 rookie season with Minnesota.

8.9   D. Four teams

Significant Hispanic populations in Los Angeles, Miami and San Francisco have provided a second and ever-growing fan base for the Kings, Mighty Ducks, Panthers and Sharks, the four NHL clubs that broadcast home games on Spanish radio. The Sharks, or *el*

Tiburones, are also seen on television, available to the 1.2 million Spanish-speaking residents in the Bay Area.

8.10 D. The St. Louis Blues

Following a 15-year NHL playing career, the last four seasons with the Blues, Arbour coached St. Louis for 107 games (42–40–25) between 1970 and 1973. He scouted briefly for the Atlanta Flames before becoming the Islanders' third coach in 1973–74. Within two years, New York was a playoff contender and before the decade ended, Arbour was named 1979's NHL coach of the year. The next season he won the Islanders' first of four-in-a-row Cups, 1980, 1981, 1982 and 1983.

8.11 B. 1984

The U.S. Olympic hockey team of 1984 had none of the gold-medal success of their predecessors four years earlier, but they did have some impressive moments, particularly from a forward unit dubbed "The Diaper Line." The mighty trio of high-school players included Pat LaFontaine, David A. Jensen and Ed Olczyk. The American team finished seventh in the standings.

8.12 A. Flyer general manager Bobby Clarke

By all press accounts the big line that dominated the NHL in 1995 came together at the suggestion of Clarke, who originally made the deal that brought the Canadiens' John LeClair, Eric Desjardins and Gilbert Dionne to Philadelphia (for 100-point man Mark Recchi and a third-round pick). But the Flyers boss readily admits that although the idea looked good on paper, he had no idea how it would work on ice, nor how productive LeClair would become once teamed with Lindros and Renberg. The chemistry was evident immediately, as LeClair was moved from his centre position to left wing by coach Murray. In 37 games, LeClair netted 25 goals and 49 points for a +21 as a brand-new Flyer.

8.13 C. The Vancouver Canucks

On February 11, 1982, Vancouver's Thomas Gradin and Ivan Hlinka each scored on third-period penalty shots against Detroit's Gilles Gilbert. Gradin's penalty shot was awarded because forward Jody Gage glove-grabbed the puck in the Red Wings crease. Hlinka's goal came after Detroit's Willie Huber hauled down Stan Smyl from behind on a breakaway. Smyl was injured, so Hlinka took the crucial penalty shot that tied the game with just 30 seconds remaining. It marked the first time one club scored two penalty-shot goals in a single game.

8.14 A. The Boston Bruins

The abundance of Bruin talent during the 1970s was never more apparent than in 1970–71, the season Phil Esposito (152 points), Bobby Orr (139 points), Johnny Bucyk (116 points) and Ken Hodge (105 points) all recorded +100-point seasons, an NHL first by one team. It was also the first time in NHL history one club sported the top four players in the point standings.

8.15 B. The Chicago Blackhawks

After wearing No. 9 for 13 NHL seasons with Los Angeles, New York, Edmonton and New Jersey, Nicholls chose No. 92 in Chicago, to honour the memory of his son, Jack, who was born with Down syndrome in 1992 (and died shortly after of spinal meningitis and pneumonia). Chicago great Bobby Hull was the Hawks' last No. 9.

8.16 C. The 1984–85 Edmonton Oilers

Led by Wayne Gretzky and Jari Kurri, the 1984–85 Oilers produced the best season start by a team in NHL history, winning 12 games and tying three for a record undefeated streak of 15 games between October 11 and November 9, 1984. The next-best streaking teams from the start of a season are the 1943–44 Canadiens (11W-

3T), the 1995 Penguins (12W-1T) and the 1972-73 Canadiens (9W-4T).

8.17 D. Five

You've heard of the home buyer's hex (once a player buys a new home, he's traded), in Ottawa, reporters are calling it the "Captain's Curse." If you're named a Senator captain, you're history. Randy Cunneyworth is the fifth Ottawa captain in two years, after Laurie Boschman, Mark Lamb, Brad Shaw and Gord Dineen, who all got ditched (for various reasons) after being struck by the jinx.

8.18 C. 25–10–3

After languishing with a 3–6–1 record, the Flyers suddenly caught fire with LeClair and defenseman Eric Desjardins on board, posting a 25–10–3 record in 38 games. The combined offensive drive of the three Legionnaires (160 points and 75 of the Flyers' 127 team goals) propelled the Flyers to the Atlantic Conference Championship, after a five-year absence from playoff action.

8.19 A. Gretzky's close friend and agent, Mike Barnett

Gretzky gave the 801 jersey to Barnett on March 20, 1994, the night he tied Howe's career point total. According to witnesses, Barnett, who had not owned a Gretzky game-worn jersey to that point, was speechless. As thanks, Barnett purchased the Pacific Coliseum net in which Gretzky scored his 802nd goal and gave it to the Great One for his Toronto restaurant.

8.20 C. 1975, the Philadelphia Flyers

Only two teams have ever had the first overall pick after finishing first: the 1969 Canadiens, who were awarded the top two French Canadian players for the last time; and the 1975 Flyers, who snagged Mel Bridgman after trading Don MacLean, Bill Clement and their 1975 first-rounder for the Washington Capitals' first overall choice. In 1971, the Canadiens finished fourth, while taking Guy Lafleur first in that year's draft; Boston selected Gord Kluzak first in 1982, after their fourth-place finish.

8.21 A. Less than three minutes
On November 22, 1972, the Pittsburgh Penguins scored the NHL's five fastest goals by one team, blasting St. Louis's Wayne Stephenson with third-period goals from Bryan Hextall at 12:00; Jean Pronovost, 12:18; Al McDonough, 13:40; Ken Schinkel, 13:49; and Ron Schock, 14:07. The five goals came in a record two minutes, seven seconds. Pittsburgh defeated St. Louis 10–4.

8.22 D. The New Jersey Devils
The Devils' Jacques Lemaire is one of the few NHL coaches to consistently play four lines each game, even in the playoffs. And after forming The Crash Line of Bobby Holik, Randy McKay and Mike Peluso in 1993–94, he made good on his four-line system, using the fourth line trio through the entire 1995 Stanley Cup. The Crash Line combined to score 23 individual points in their post-season championship.

8.23 D. Bergeron for cash and a New York first-round pick
On paper, the match was ingenious. Bring hockey's most colourful bench boss to the NHL's loudest and most vibrant city. Bring the scrappy, blood-boiling Bergeron to cosmopolitan, sports-mad New York to coach the Rangers. Esposito thought he had found the right man at the right time to spark his struggling team. So, in June 1987, Espo "traded" $100,000 and the Rangers' 1988 first-round draft pick to Quebec for the Nords' heart and soul, the feisty Bergeron, known as "*le petit tigre*," or "Little Tiger." The Esposito-Bergeron tandem didn't last long, though. The men were too similar,

and Bergeron was gone from New York after less than two seasons, replaced by Espo himself.

8.24 C. Johnny Bucyk's No. 9

Ever since he began playing organized hockey in his native Quebec, Juneau's favourite jersey number was No. 9. As a kid, he'd always arrive early to get the first sweater pick. But in Boston, No. 9 was hanging from the rafters, retired after the 21-year career of Bruin great Johnny Bucyk. So Juneau asked Bucyk if he would mind "unretiring" his No. 9. Bucyk happily agreed, but on the condition that Juneau hand over his six-figure signing bonus. Juneau, ever the creative hockey mind, laughed along with Bucyk at the proposal, but came up with No. 49, in honour of Bobby Orr's No. 4 and Bucyk's No. 9.

8.25 D. The Chicago Blackhawks

During their 24 home games in 1995's abbreviated season, the Blackhawks averaged 20,810 fans at the new United Center, up from 17,776 in the final season at Chicago Stadium.

8.26 B. The Canada Cup in 1976

It was an emotional moment few will forget. At the Montreal Forum, in sudden-death overtime, Canada defeats the defending world champion Czech team on a goal by Darryl Sittler. After the ceremonial handshakes, a group of Czechs corral Bobby Orr, slapping him on his back and tugging at their own sweaters. In one spontaneous act of true sportsmanship, players exchanged team jerseys. Bob Gainey slipped on Frantisek Pospisil's No. 7; Rogie Vachon exchanged No. 1s with Vladimir Dzurilla; and Sittler traded his No. 27 to get Bohuslav Ebermann's No. 25.

GAME 8

FIRST-ON-THE-TEAM 50-GOAL MEN

From the stars listed below, select the 22 NHLers who became their team's first 50-goal men and place their names opposite the club on which they established the feat. (We'll count Atlanta and Calgary as two teams in this case; likewise for Minnesota and Dallas.)

(Solutions are on page 118)

Teemu Selanne	Brett Hull	Mike Bossy
Michel Goulet	Lanny McDonald	Jacques Richard
Rick Martin	Pierre Larouche	Rick Vaive
Dale Hawerchuk	Wayne Babych	Brian Bellows
Denis Maruk	Maurice Richard	Al Secord
Marcel Dionne	Ken Hodge	Phil Esposito
Reggie Leach	Guy Chouinard	Pavel Bure
Dino Ciccarelli	Danny Gare	Rick MacLeish
Bobby Hull	Wayne Gretzky	Blaine Stoughton
Mickey Redmond	Vic Hadfield	Bryan Trottier
Mike Modano	Jean Pronovost	Andy Bathgate

CANADIENS (1945): _____   HAWKS (1962): _____

BRUINS (1971): _____   RANGERS (1972): _____

RED WINGS (1973): _____   FLYERS (1973): _____

SABRES (1974): _____   PENGUINS (1976): _____

KINGS (1977): _____   ISLES (1978): _____

ATLANTA (1979): _____   WHALERS (1980): _____

OILERS (1980): _____   BLUES (1981): _____

NORDIQUES (1981): _____   CAPITALS (1981): _____

MINNESOTA (1982): _____   LEAFS (1982): _____

FLAMES (1983): _____   JETS (1985): _____

CANUCKS (1993): _____   STARS (1993): _____

9

TRUE OR FALSE TURNOVERS

The neutral-zone trap is a defensive strategy that creates turnovers at centre ice by forcing puck carriers towards the boards. Its success is dependent on good forechecking and smart passing, which quickly turn defense into superior offense and lead to two-on-one and three-on-two advantages.

Before we head into the playoffs and our Stanley Cup chapter, we hit some speeding rushers in the neutral zone to create a few giveaways of our own. How well you do here could be determined by how closely you've paid attention to the facts in previous chapters.

(Answers are on page 99)

9.1 Wayne Gretzky scored his 2,500th point in less than 1,000 games. *True or False?*

9.2 According to *National Hockey League Official Rules*, there is no area of the rink where a player is allowed to direct a puck to a teammate with his hand. *True or False?*

9.3 No defenseman has ever scored 50 goals in regular-season play. *True or False?*

9.4 John LeClair is the biggest member of The Legion of Doom. *True or False?*

9.5 Despite being one of the NHL's oldest teams, the New York Rangers have only retired two uniform numbers. The players who wore them both starred in the 1960s and 1970s. *True or False?*

9.6 Only two defensemen have ever reached the 40-goal plateau in regular-season play. *True or False?*

9.7 Since 1927, when the NHL took sole possession of the Stanley Cup, no post-season has ever concluded without at least one overtime playoff game. *True or False?*

9.8 Pittsburgh's Mario Lemieux scored more goals in his first three seasons than Pavel Bure did in Vancouver. *True or False?*

9.9 Among all NHL teams, the last-place Ottawa Senators allowed Eric Lindros the fewest points during the truncated 1995 regular season. *True or False?*

9.10 Except for when Sergei Zubov led the first-place (overall) New York Rangers in scoring in 1993–94, no other regular-season champions have had a defenseman as top team scorer. *True or False?*

9.11 The only time a referee can disallow a goal because of an illegal stick is when the goal is scored on a penalty shot. *True or False?*

9.12 No *three* players have ever tied in the regular-season points standings in one year. *True or False?*

9.13 Wayne Gretzky is the only NHLer to wear No. 99 on an NHL hockey sweater. *True or False?*

9.14 No NHLer ever signed with all six teams of the Original Six era. *True or False?*

9.15 Joe Juneau is the only 100-point rookie to *not* win the Calder Trophy as NHL Rookie of the Year. *True or False?*

9.16 The former home of the Quebec Nordiques, Colisée de Québec has two Stanley Cup banners hanging from its rafters. *True or False?*

9.17 A defenseman (rather than a forward) holds the NHL record for most assists in one game. *True or False?*

9.18 Glenn Hall never played a single overtime game during his 552 consecutive game streak between 1955 and 1962. *True or False?*

9.19 No goal is scored if the puck is deflected into the net off an official. *True or False?*

9.20 No two goalies from different teams have ever shared the Vezina Trophy (best goaltender) in the same year. *True or False?*

9.21 The first U.S.-born player to score 200 goals was a defenseman. *True or False?*

9.22 Wayne Gretzky was the youngest player to win the Hart Trophy as league MVP. *True or False?*

9.23 No Maple Leaf has ever won the Conn Smythe Trophy as playoff MVP. *True or False?*

9.24 Lord Stanley of Preston, donator of the Stanley Cup, is the only "Stanley" on hockey's championship trophy. *True or False?*

TRUE OR FALSE TURNOVERS
Answers

9.1 False

Gretzky reached the 2,500-point plateau on a Rob Blake goal on April 17, 1995. It was his 1,165th NHL game.

9.2 False

Hand passes—hit in the air or along the ice—are only permitted in the defender's zone. Anywhere else, the play is whistled down and the face-off occurs where the infraction took place.

9.3 True

The closest any NHL rearguard has ever come to scoring 50 goals in one season is Paul Coffey's 48-goal year in 1985–86, two better than Orr's 46-goal season in 1974–75.

9.4 False

Eric Lindros is the biggest Legionnaire, at six foot four, 229 pounds, followed by Mikael Renberg (six foot two, 218 pounds) and John LeClair (six foot two, 215 pounds).

9.5 True

Since 1927, many Ranger greats, such as Andy Bathgate, Brad Park and Vic Hadfield, have donned the famous New York blueshirt, but only Eddie Giacomin's No. 1 and Rod Gilbert's No. 7 have been retired.

9.6 True

Only Bobby Orr and Paul Coffey (twice) have ever scored 40 or more goals in a season. Doug Wilson's valiant effort in 1981–82 fell one goal short.

9.7 False

The only playoff year without any overtime games was 1963. None of the 16 post-season games required extra periods. Toronto won their best-of-seven semi-final series defeating Montreal 4–1; Detroit beat Chicago in six in their match-up; and during the finals, the Maple Leafs easily handled the Red Wings, winning the Stanley Cup in five games. Of the 16 playoff matches, only three games were decided by one goal.

9.8 False

Bure (154 goals) has the NHL's third-highest first three-year goal-totals, behind Wayne Gretzky (198) and Mike Bossy (173), but ahead of Joe Nieuwendyk's 147-goal count and Mario, who scored 145 goals in his first three seasons.

9.9 True

In three games against the hopeless Senators, Lindros collected his lowest point totals, only one goal and one assist, helping Ottawa compile a 2–1–0 record over the Atlantic Division champion Flyers. While the Senators insisted nothing special had been done to curb No. 88, it's clear Lindros saved his best for the best teams, scoring five points in three matches against Pittsburgh and six points in four games against the Nordiques.

9.10 False

After the Rangers and Zubov did it in 1993–94, the 1995 Detroit Red Wings became the second team in as many years (and in NHL history) to finish in first place overall with a blueliner as team scoring leader. Paul Coffey led the Wings with 58 points.

9.11 True

A goal on a penalty shot is the only time officials can disallow a goal because of an illegal stick. The rule received considerable attention from general managers after a February 10, 1995, incident involving the Panthers' Petr Klima, who purposely snapped his stick at the blade in order to prevent a stick measurement. The request by Hartford followed Klima's game-winning goal in the 4–3 Florida win. But no matter whether the stick was legal or not, the goal stood according to *National Hockey League Official Rules* (Section three, Rule 20 (e)). It's a rule many general managers feel needs reworking. Klima was assessed a two-minute unsportsmanlike-conduct penalty and an automatic 10-minute misconduct.

9.12 True

Although two players have tied for the scoring title on three separate occasions, three players have never shared the top spot in regular-season point totals.

9.13 False

In the modern era, both Wilf Paiement of Toronto and the Jets' Rick Dudley have donned 99s.

9.14 False

Bronco Horvath is the only NHLer during the six-team era to have signed with Detroit (though he did not play), New York, Montreal, Boston, Chicago and Toronto.

9.15 True

Among the five NHL rookies who have scored 100 points, only Juneau failed to capture the Calder as top rookie. Blame Teemu Selanne, whose phenomenal freshman season coincided with Juneau's.

THE NHL'S ONLY 100-POINT ROOKIES

Player	Team	Season	GP	G	A	PTS
T. Selanne*	Jets	1992–93	84	76	56	132
P. Stastny*	Nords	1980–81	77	39	70	109
D. Hawerchuk*	Jets	1981–82	80	45	58	103
J. Juneau	Bruins	1992–93	84	32	70	102
M. Lemieux*	Pens	1984–85	73	43	57	100

Calder Trophy winner / Current to 1995.

9.16 True

In pre-NHL days, the Quebec Bulldogs, with Hall-of-Famers Paddy Moran, Joe Hall and Joe Malone, were a force, winning back-to-back Cups in 1912–13 and 1913–14. Those two championship years are honoured with banners at Le Colisée, hung by a hockey-starved city that will probably not see NHL action again for a long time.

9.17 False

Forwards Billy Taylor (1947) and Wayne Gretzky (1980, 1985, 1986) are the only NHLers to score seven assists in a single game, just one more than a bunch of players with six assists, including defensemen Babe Pratt, Bobby Orr and Paul Coffey.

9.18 False

Since there was no regular-season overtime during Hall's era, the only occasion for extra periods was in playoff action. In 49 post-season games (during his 552-game streak), Hall played 65 minutes, 12 seconds of overtime, winning two of three games. In Detroit's 5–4 win over Toronto on March 24, 1956, Hall played 4:22 of overtime; in the March 26, 1960 Chicago, 4–3 loss to Montreal, he went 8:38; and in the Blackhawks' 2–1 marathon victory against Montreal on March 26, 1961, Hall survived 52:12 of OT.

9.19 True

According to Rule 55 (e) of *National Hockey League Official Rules*, a goal is disallowed if the puck deflects into the net off an official.

9.20 False

The only tie in Vezina Trophy history happened in 1973–74, when both Chicago and Philadelphia allowed 164 goals, producing a tie for top goalie honours between Tony Esposito and Bernie Parent.

9.21 True

Bruins defenseman Reed Larson of Minneapolis, Minnesota, became the first American-born player to score 200 NHL goals in a 6–4 win over the Hartford Whalers on January 15, 1987. Larson, who logged most of his goals working on the Detroit blueline, recorded goal number 200 just one month before New York-born Joe Mullen's 200th, February 14, 1987.

9.22 True

Gretzky became the youngest NHLer to capture the NHL's MVP honours when he was just 19 years, five months old, in June 1980.

9.23 False

Only one Toronto player has ever won the award named in honour of Maple Leaf builder and founder, the great Conn Smythe. Dave Keon copped the playoff MVP trophy in 1967, when the Leafs defeated Montreal in the finals, 4–2.

9.24 False

Three other Stanleys have had their names inscribed on the Cup since Lord Stanley first donated the trophy in 1892: Barney Stanley of the Vancouver Millionaires, 1915; Allan Stanley of the Toronto Maple Leafs, 1962, 1963, 1964 and 1967; and executive Stanley Jaffe of the New York Rangers, 1994.

GAME 9

"WELCOME TO HELL!"

The 1995 Stanley Cup finals were a surprise to most hockey observers, including the Cup-finalist Detroit Red Wings. After a near-perfect three playoff rounds, the heavily-favoured Red Wings got clipped by the neutral-zoning New Jersey Devils in two home games at Joe Louis Arena. Down 0–2, the Red Wings took to the ice for game three at the Meadowlands Arena to face a Devils crowd sporting Satan costumes, demonic horns and spectator signboards. One read: "Welcome To Hell!" It was an omen of the inferno about to engulf the Red Wings, who got burned by the Cup-winning Devils in four straight.

In this game, the challenge is to match the hometown arenas with their real-life spectator signboards. Each slogan represents a hockey event from 1995.

(Solutions are on page 118)

St. Louis's Kiel Center   Vancouver's Pacific Coliseum
San Jose Arena   Philadelphia's Spectrum
Boston Garden   New Jersey's Meadowlands Arena
Montreal Forum   Pittsburgh's Civic Arena
Winnipeg Arena   Colisée de Québec
New York's Madison Square
    Garden

1._____ "GOlf HABS GOlf."
2._____ "Its A *Hull* Of A Night."
3._____ "Hey Nashville! You Can Have The Red Wings."
4._____ "Save Our Jets."
5._____ "HEXcellent."
6._____ "Adieu, Nos Nords."
7._____ "Here Lies The Capitals. Put To Rest By The Best."
8._____ "Thanks For All The Memories. And All The Good Times. Goodbye Garden."
9._____ "Keenan Sucks."
10._____ "Now I Can Die In Peace."
11._____ "What Do Sharks Eat For Breakfast? Calgary Flames."

10

SYMPATHY FOR THE DEVILS

After the NHL's worst labour dispute reduced the 1994–95 regular season to 48 games, it was almost expected that more weirdness would follow in post-season. The 1995 Stanley Cup-winning New Jersey Devils didn't disappoint. They were perhaps the most unusual Cup victors ever. Winning with their much-maligned defensive system, the Devils dressed more Americans than Canadians, an NHL first; played a local hero one game and scratched him the next; and held their Stanley Cup parade in a Jersey parking lot as fans screamed "Nashville sucks," after rumours of a franchise move to Tennessee. Bizarre. In this chapter, our chase for the chalice follows a more traditional route (with a few exceptions).

(Answers are on page 109)

10.1 **What team holds the record for most consecutive appearances in the playoffs?**
A. The Detroit Red Wings
B. The Boston Bruins
C. The Montreal Canadiens
D. The Toronto Maple Leafs

10.2 **Who was the first player in NHL history to score back-to-back Stanley Cup-winning goals?**
A. Jean Béliveau
B. Ron Francis
C. Wayne Gretzky
D. Mike Bossy

10.3 Since 1987, when each of the four playoff series required best-of-seven formats, what championship team won the Stanley Cup in the fewest number of post-season games? And how many games were played, if the minimum is 16 matches and the maximum is 28?
A. The 1988 Edmonton Oilers
B. The 1991 Pittsburgh Penguins
C. The 1993 Montreal Canadiens
D. The 1995 New Jersey Devils

10.4 How many players from the 1995 Stanley Cup-winning New Jersey Devils played for the Colorado Rockies before that team moved its franchise to New Jersey in 1982?
A. None
B. One
C. Two
D. Three

10.5 What Stanley Cup-winning team from Montreal is missing championship banners in its home arena?
A. The Montreal Wanderers
B. The Montreal Maroons
C. The Montreal Canadiens
D. The Montreal Victorias

10.6 What is the most number of goals scored by one individual in one playoff year?
A. 15
B. 17
C. 19
D. 21

10.7 **Which Stanley Cup ring does Scotty Bowman wear?**
A. His first, the Canadiens' 1973 championship ring
B. His third, the Canadiens' 1977 championship ring
C. His sixth, the Penguins' 1991 championship ring
D. His seventh, the Penguins' 1992 championship ring

10.8 **How many American-born players were on the 1995 Stanley Cup champion New Jersey Devils?**
A. Eight
B. 10
C. 12
D. 14

10.9 **Whose post-season career points record did Wayne Gretzky beat when he scored his 177th playoff point in 1987?**
A. Gordie Howe
B. Jean Béliveau
C. Stan Mikita
D. Henri Richard

10.10 **Who was the first goalie in NHL history to score a goal in playoff competition?**
A. Ron Hextall
B. Darcy Wakaluk
C. Billy Smith
D. Bob Froese

10.11 **Which American-born player on the 1995 Cup-winning New Jersey Devils scored a game-winning goal one game and was benched the next?**
A. Brian Rolston
B. Tom Chorske
C. Bill Guerin
D. Jim Dowd

10.12 Who broke Maurice Richard's playoff career goal-scoring record first?
A. Jari Kurri
B. Glenn Anderson
C. Mike Bossy
D. Wayne Gretzky

10.13 Who is the only forward from a losing club to win the Conn Smythe as playoff MVP?
A. St. Louis' Red Berenson
B. The Islanders' Butch Goring
C. Montreal's Bob Gainey
D. Philadelphia's Reggie Leach

SYMPATHY FOR THE DEVILS
Answers

10.1   B. The Boston Bruins
The Bruins have participated in every NHL post-season between 1968 and 1995, a record 28 playoff appearances and the longest streak among all teams in North American professional sport. Although they are one of the NHL's most consistent regular-season teams (23 first- or second-place finishes in their division), during their 28-year playoff stretch Boston has won only two Stanley Cups and has lost the Cup finals five times.

10.2   D. Mike Bossy
Béliveau did score two Cup winners (1960 and 1965), but only Bossy notched his championship duo in back-to-back post-seasons, eliminating the Vancouver Canucks in 1982 and the Edmonton Oilers in 1983.

10.3　A. The 1988 Edmonton Oilers

The Gretzky-led Oilers won the 1988 Stanley Cup in 18 games, losing just twice during their best-of-seven, four-round playoff series, once to Winnipeg in the Division semi-finals and another in the Conference finals to the Red Wings. Edmonton won the other two series, the Division finals against Calgary and the Cup finals versus Boston, both in four games straight.

10.4　A. None

Ironically, the last Rockie to play with New Jersey was Aaron Broten, kid brother of 1995 Cup-winning Devil, Neal Broten. Aaron played one season with Colorado before the team moved to New Jersey, where he stayed seven years until his trade to the Minnesota North Stars on January 5, 1990. Brother Neal had better timing, coming to the Devils mid-season from Minnesota's successor, the Dallas Stars, in 1995. The longest surviving Devils to become 1995 Cup champions are Ken Daneyko, Bruce Driver and John MacLean, who began their NHL careers in New Jersey in 1983–84, the Devils' second NHL season.

10.5　B. The Montreal Maroons

Montreal teams like the Victorias, Wanderers and Maroons were all multiple Cup winners in hockey's early days, but only the Maroons' home arena still survives, and without any championship banners to recognize their two Stanley Cup victories in 1926 and 1935. The reason? The Maroons' home rink was the Montreal Forum. Contrary to popular thought, the famous arena was built for the Maroons (not the Canadiens), and even though the 1926 team won the first Cup awarded in the arena, no banners hang in their honour. The Canadiens fans wouldn't stand for it.

10.6   C. 19

Reggie Leach and Jari Kurri share the record for most goals in one playoff season, each scoring 19 times in respective years, 1976 and 1985. Leach registered his 19 goals in 16 games, while Kurri needed 18 matches.

10.7   C. His sixth, the Penguins' 1991 championship ring

Although Bowman has coached six Stanley Cup winners, five with Montreal and one with Pittsburgh, he only wears the Penguins' championship ring from 1991, the year the late Bob Johnson coached and Scotty was director of player development. Bowman likes the fit and says it's not as "big" as his other Stanley Cup rings.

10.8   C. 12

Never before has a Stanley Cup-winning team featured so many American players. There were a record eight U.S.-born NHLers on the 1938 Chicago Blackhawks, but the 1995 Devils topped that mark with 12 Americans: Neal Broten, Bobby Carpenter, Tom Chorske, Jim Dowd, Bill Guerin, Chris Terreri, Mike Peluso, Shawn Chambers, Brian Rolston, Dayton Cole, Kevin Dean and Chris McAlpine. For those patriots who keep count, there were also nine Canadians and four Europeans.

10.9   B. Jean Béliveau

When Gretzky recorded his 177th playoff point from a Jari Kurri goal on April 9, 1987, he had broken the 16-year-old record of Jean Béliveau, who amassed a playoff career total of 176 points (79G-97A) upon retirement in 1971. It was the Great One's 82nd playoff game; Big Jean took 162 games.

10.10 A. Ron Hextall

The NHL's first playoff goal by a netminder came during the fifth game of the Patrick Division semi-finals on April 11, 1989. Late in the game, with the Flyers short-handed on a penalty, the Capitals pull Pete Peeters for the extra attacker. Hextall gathers the puck and starts thinking "Goal." He launches the puck 180 feet into the Washington's empty net. All Peeters could do was watch from the bench as Hextall's shorthanded empty-netter wrapped up Philadelphia's 8–5 win.

10.11 D. Jim Dowd

With the score tied 2–2 and fewer than two minutes remaining in game two of the 1995 Red Wings-Devils finals, New Jersey-native Dowd, a late add-on to the lineup, picked up a rebound and with Mike Vernon down bulged the net for the game winner. (Paul Coffey was out of the play after being hit by a Bill Guerin shot.) The next game, played in Dowd's home state of New Jersey, the local hero was benched, which, accord-ing to Dowd, is "just the way it is on this team."

10.12 C. Mike Bossy

It took 26 years of post-season play before anyone beat the Rocket's career record for most goals during the playoffs. Richard's 82-goal mark, set in 1960, was final-ly eclipsed during the 1986 playoffs by Bossy, who scored his 83rd career goal against the Capitals' Pete Peeters on April 12, 1986. Bossy's career record of 85 playoff goals was surpassed by Wayne Gretzky during the 1989 post-season.

10.13 D. Philadelphia's Reggie Leach

The 1976 Stanley Cup is most often remembered for its final series, a confrontation between two teams with distinctly different playing styles: the strong-armed tac-tics of Philadelphia's Broad Street Bullies versus the finesse and indestructible defense of Montreal's Flying

Frenchmen. The 4–0 series win by the Canadiens was considered by many a signpost of the game's future. Clean playmaking would prevail over dirty hockey. Ironically, it was a member of the "bullying" Flyers who set a couple of offensive records that playoff year and came away with MVP honours. Leach, playing on the Flyers' top line with Bobby Clarke and Bill Barber, scored a record 19 goals in 16 playoff games and established the longest consecutive goal-scoring streak in one post-season—nine games. Despite going down in four straight to Montreal, Leach was named playoff MVP, the only forward from a losing team to win the Conn Smythe.

SOLUTIONS TO GAMES

GAME 1: THE PINWHEEL PUCK

GAME 2: ROOKIES—THE HONOUR ROLL

1995	Peter Forsberg	Jim Carey
1994	Martin Brodeur	Jason Arnott
1993	Teemu Selanne	Joe Juneau
1992	Pavel Bure	Nicklas Lidstrom
1991	Ed Belfour	Sergei Fedorov
1990	Sergei Makarov	Mike Modano
1989	Brian Leetch	Trevor Linden
1988	Joe Nieuwendyk	Ray Sheppard
1987	Luc Robtaille	Ron Hextall
1986	Gary Suter	Wendel Clark
1985	Mario Lemieux	Chris Chelios
1984	Tom Barrasso	Steve Yzerman

GAME 3: THE 20-YEAR MEN

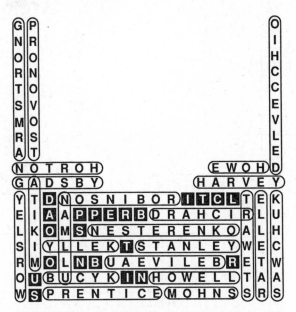

Dit Clapper of the **Boston Bruins** became the first NHLer to play 20 seasons, scoring 228 goals and 246 assists for 474 points between 1927-28 and 1946-47. Clapper, a career Bruin, played forward and defense, his best season coming in 1929-30, when he scored 41 goals in 44 games. He won three Stanley Cups and was named to first and second All-Star teams on three occasions.

GAME 4: WAYNE GRETZKY—YEAR BY YEAR

1. 1979	5. 1981	9. 1994	13. 1987
2. 1991	6. 1993	10. 1989	14. 1992
3. 1988	7. 1986	11. 1990	15. 1984
4. 1985	8. 1983	12. 1982	16. 1980

GAME 5: THE CROSSWORD

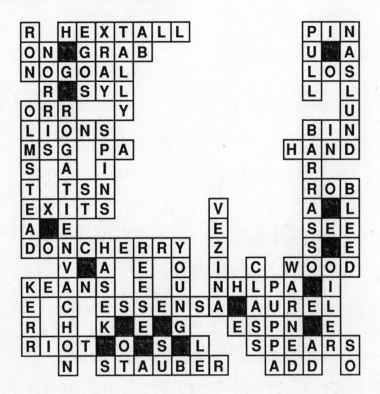

GAME 6: "LET'S SEE IF THEY KICK ME OFF THE ICE!"

Part 1	Part 2
1. Wendel Clark	1. Bob Berry
2. Harry Neale	2. Jason Arnott
3. Harold Ballard	3. Barry Melrose
4. Marcel Aubut	4. Gilbert Perreault
5. Pat Burns	5. Jamie Baker
6. Pat Flatley	6. Mike Keane
7. Brett Hull	7. Mike Keenan

GAME 7: NUMBER ONE DRAFT PICKS

Guy Lafleur   Owen Nolan   Eric Lindros
Bobby Smith   Mario Lemieux   Mats Sundin
Denis Potvin   Gord Kluzak   Roman Hamrlik
Dale Hawerchuk   Joe Murphy   Oleg Tverdovsky
Alexandre Daigle   Mike Modano   Gilbert Perreault

GAME 8: FIRST-ON-THE-TEAM 50-GOAL MEN

CANADIENS:	Maurice Richard	HAWKS:	Bobby Hull
BRUINS:	Phil Esposito	RANGERS:	Vic Hadfield
RED WINGS:	Mickey Redmond	FLYERS:	Rick MacLeish
SABRES:	Rick Martin	PENGUINS:	Jean Pronovost
KINGS:	Marcel Dionne	ISLANDERS:	Mike Bossy
ATLANTA:	Guy Chouinard	WHALERS:	Blaine Stoughton
OILERS:	Wayne Gretzky	BLUES:	Wayne Babych
NORDIQUES:	Jacques Richard	CAPITALS:	Dennis Maruk
MINNESOTA:	Dino Ciccarelli	LEAFS:	Rich Vaive
FLAMES:	Lanny McDonald	JETS:	Dale Hawerchuk
CANUCKS:	Pavel Bure	STARS:	Mike Modano

GAME 9: "WELCOME TO HELL!"

1. Montreal Forum
Golf comes unusually early for the Canadiens. For the first time in 25 years Montreal fails to make the playoffs.

2. St. Louis's Kiel Center
Blues fans celebrate two first-period goals by Brett Hull, who leads St. Louis to an 8–2 win over the Vancouver Canucks in game six of the Conference quarter-finals. The Blues strike a sour note in game seven and lose to the Canucks, 5-3.

3. New Jersey's Meadowlands Arena
Fans of the Stanley Cup champion Devils propose an alternative to the rumours of a New Jersey franchise move to Nashville: send the Devils' opponents, the Cup-losing finalist Red Wings, to Tennessee.

4. Winnipeg Arena
Jets fans protest the proposed sale of their team to Minnesota.

5. Philadelphia's Spectrum

Flyer fans get creative as goalie Ron Hextall gets excellent, stopping 31 of 33 shots to defeat the New Jersey Devils in game three of the Conference finals.

6. Colisée de Québec

Guessing that it may be the last game the Nordiques play in Québec, fans bid goodbye on May 14, 1995. The Nords beat the Rangers 4–2 but lose the next Conference quarter-final game and the series in New York. Weeks later the Quebec team is sold to Denver.

7. Pittsburgh's Civic Arena

The Penguins finally put the last nail into Washington's playoff coffin, winning in seven games in the Conference quarter-finals and advancing to the semi-finals against the Devils.

8. Boston Garden

On May 14, 1995 (the same night as the Nords' final game in Quebec), Boston fans said goodbye for the last time to the Garden, home of the Bruins since 1928.

9. Vancouver's Pacific Coliseum

Canuck fans make no apologies and let Blues coach Mike Keenan know how they really feel.

10. New York's Madison Square Garden

Ranger fans sport T-shirts and placards that celebrate 1994's Stanley Cup. Unfortunately, Eric Lindros and the Flyers have other ideas and defeat New York to advance to the Conference finals.

11. San Jose Arena

The underdog Sharks come through again with a playoff upset, this time eliminating the first-place Flames in the Conference quarter-finals, 5–4 in a seventh game overtime victory.

ACKNOWLEDGEMENTS

Care has been taken to trace ownership of copyright material contained in this book. The publishers welcome any information that will enable them to rectify any reference or credit in subsequent editions.

The author gratefully acknowledges the help of Wayne Hicks; Lynn Hoffman of the Hackensack Medical Centre; Les Bowen of the *Philadelphia News; Canadian Hockey;* Steve Dryden of *the Hockey News;* the Sweden National Post Office; the *Los Angeles Daily News;* Phil Pritchard and Craig Campbell at the Hockey Hall of Fame; the staff at the McLellan-Redpath Library at McGill University; Ron Reusch and Rob Faulds of CFCF-12 in Montreal; Robert Clements at Greystone Books; the many hockey writers and broadcasters who have made the game better through their own work; as well as my editors Kerry Banks and Anne Rose, fact checker Allen Bishop, graphic artist Ivor Tiltin and puzzle designer Adrian van Vlaardingen.

HOCKEY TRIVIA'S READER REBOUND

Do you have a favourite hockey trivia question that stumps everyone? Or one that needs an answer? Write us, and if we haven't used it before, we may include it in next year's trivia book. We can only pick about 20 questions and answers, so give us your best shot.

We'll make sure every question selected is credited with the sender's name and city. Just two points: 1) Duplications will be decided by earliest postmark; and 2) Sorry, we can't answer letters individually.

Write us at: HOCKEY TRIVIA
c/o DON WEEKES
P.O. BOX 221
MONTREAL, QUEBEC
CANADA
H4A 3P5

Please print

NAME: _____ AGE: _____

ADDRESS: _____

_____

FAVOURITE TEAM:

_____

FAVOURITE PLAYER(S): _____

_____

YOUR QUESTION: _____

_____

_____

_____

_____

ANSWER: _____

_____

_____

_____

_____

_____

_____

(continued on next page)

Even if you don't have a trivia question, we'd like to hear from you.

READER SURVEY

In future books on hockey trivia, would you like questions that are:

Easier _____   About the same _____   Harder _____

Would you like more games _____ ;   or fewer games _____

What kinds of questions or games do you like the most, or would like more of? (i.e., multiple choice, true or false, fill-in-the-blanks, crosswords, etc.) _____
_____
_____
_____

OTHER COMMENTS: _____
_____
_____
_____
_____
_____

THE OPINION CORNER

What do you like most about hockey? _____
_____
_____

How would you like the game to change: (i.e., shootouts, two referees, etc.) _____
_____
_____

When and how did you first get interested in hockey?
_____
_____
_____